WILLIAM CAREY

Father of Missions

Sam Wellman

BARBOUR
PUBLISHING, INC.
Uhrichsville, Ohio

Other books in the "Heroes of the Faith" series:

Gladys Aylward

Brother Andrew

Corrie ten Boom

William and Catherine Booth

John Bunyan

Amy Carmichael

George Washington Carver

Fanny Crosby

Frederick Douglass

Jonathan Edwards

Jim Elliot

Charles Finney

Billy Graham

C. S. Lewis

Eric Liddell

David Livingstone

Martin Luther

D. L. Moody

Samuel Morris

George Müller

Watchman Nee

John Newton

Florence Nightingale

Mary Slessor

Charles Spurgeon

Hudson Taylor

Mother Teresa

Sojourner Truth

John Wesley

©MCMXCVII by Sam Wellman

ISBN 1-57748-106-2

Published by Barbour Publishing, Inc., P.O. Box 719, Uhrichsville, Ohio 44683
http://www.barbourbooks.com

Cover illustration © Dick Bobnick

ᏋᏟᎮᎯ Member of the
Evangelical Christian
Publishers Association

Printed in the United States of America.

WILLIAM CAREY

*To the memory of
Leonard Wellman*

one

*I*t was Uncle Peter who made the English village of Paulerspury seem small to six-year-old Willy Carey in 1767. All his uncle's talk about far-off places seemed blather to Willy until Uncle Peter took him to a hill rising to the west beyond Paulerspury, even beyond the village of Towcester. They trudged up the hill and Uncle Peter sat him down facing north across the wide green valley of the River Nene. Windmills dotted the rolling lowlands. A blue-green waterway slashed across the valley.

"Do you see beyond the Great Canal, even beyond the town of Northampton to that green rise on the far horizon, lad?" asked Uncle Peter.

"Beyond Northampton? Yes, I think so, sir." It wasn't much, that vague green thing.

"It weren't but a mite over one hundred years ago—your Great-great-grandpa Carey was there—that two great armies faced each other near the village of Naseby."

"We English against the French dogs?" asked Willy expectantly. Didn't England always fight the French, whoever they were?

"No, lad, it was the Civil War. Englishman against Englishman. The army of King Charles fought the army of Oliver Cromwell. Ten thousand men on each side. Here. I'll show you. I don't have time to round up that many sticks, so you will have to use your imagination." Uncle Peter gathered twenty sticks. He laid down a line of ten facing another line of ten. "Now then, let me explain. . ."

Willy blurted, "Each stick is one thousand. Ten groups of ten groups of ten men." Numbers came easily to Willy.

"By Jove!" Uncle Peter blinked. "Where was I? Oh, yes. Right here in the middle of these sticks on both sides are thousands of soldiers called pikemen and musketeers. They're all decked out in a colorful vest over a white long-sleeved shirt with a wide collar. And each wears knee pants, white stockings and shiny black shoes—shoes that were probably made right here in the neighborhood of Northampton since we make most of the shoes in England. . ."

"Why is that?"

Uncle Peter winced as if he didn't want to stop to answer that question. "Why, it's because we have plenty of water and oaks for tanning leather, I suppose. And the goods can be moved around easily by river and the Great Canal. Where was I in my story? Oh, yes. At their waist the pikemen and musketeers carry a long sword in a scabbard. On their heads they wear a steel helmet."

"Dressed so fine?"

"Yes. A soldier's got to look nice. The pikeman naturally carries a pike, a spear as sharp as your father's razor and as tall as a house. And for more protection than just a helmet he wears tassets over his thighs, and plates over his chest and back—all of heavy steel. The musketeer doesn't wear all that metal. He's got to be able to move around better. Besides he's carrying a matchlock musket and musket balls and other equipment. . ."

Uncle Peter talked on and on. Willy's head swam with weapons and warhorses and cavaliers with floppy feather-plumed hats and regimental battle flags of all the colors of the rainbow. Then Uncle Peter told him about the battle. Horsemen fought horsemen. Foot soldiers fought foot soldiers. Then the horsemen on one side attacked the foot soldiers on the other side. It was all very confusing. Finally Oliver Cromwell's army beat the army of King Charles.

"But how could such a thing be, Uncle Peter?" puzzled Willy. "Nothing happens around here now. . ."

"Sometimes you have to go where things are happening."

"Canada?" asked Willy, knowing Uncle Peter had been a soldier himself in such a place before he came back to work in gardens and fields.

"Yes."

"Where is Canada?"

"Far, far to the west across a sea so vast it takes weeks to cross it in a ship."

"Were you in a battle there?"

"Yes. We fought for General James Wolfe—against the French dogs. They threatened our English colonies—what we call 'America.' " He pointed at the small sticks again. "There were nine thousand of us. See, nine of these sticks, each one. . ."

"One thousand. . ."

"It was summer. We sailed down the Saint Lawrence River and camped close to Quebec, the most important French fort in Canada. If we captured it we knew the French dogs were beaten. We fought them once in front of their fort but we couldn't break through. We camped for a long time while General Wolfe tried to figure out what to do before winter set in. Finally, 5,000 of us sailed down the river past Quebec and scaled a cliff to a high flat area called the Plain of Abraham.

9

We surprised the French at Quebec. That was the end of the French dogs in Canada, lad."

"You don't sound happy about it," observed Willy.

"I lost some good friends in that battle. Even General Wolfe died. And I'm not so sure our colonists in America aren't going to fight us Englishmen next."

At that moment Willy saw a pale green butterfly land and fold its wings. "Look, Uncle Peter. See the black dot on each wing?"

"I know that one only too well. Too bad she won't stay up here in the heights. Her greedy children—fat green caterpillars they are—love cabbages. Any gardener knows that one."

Willy liked his uncle very much. Uncle Peter had come back from Canada just about the time Grandmother Carey had died. Somehow his uncle, with his enthusiastic stories of far-off lands and love for the outdoors around Paulerspury, made her death easier to accept. They had buried her right in the churchyard next to Grandpa, who had died way back in 1743. And right next to Grandpa was Willy's other uncle, William. Willy was named after Uncle William, so he knew his father—Edmund he was called—must have loved him very much.

Willy had two sisters. Ann was four years old. Willy tried to take Ann with him into the fields but she got bored too soon with his bugs and plants and always wanted to go back. So now he went alone or with Uncle Peter. Baby sister Polly seemed to like the bugs and plants he brought back from the fields as much as he did but she was too young to toddle after him yet. Willy's mother was a mild woman who hummed while she toiled about their thatched cottage. She spent many hours at the hearth, cooking or even boiling clothes.

Naturally, Willy asked her, "Why must we boil our clothing?"

His mother glanced about as if to make sure his younger sisters were not near. "Because sometimes we share them with crawlies."

Mother spent much time baking bread, which barely cooled before Father Carey was slicing it on a small table. At meals the Careys sat on benches on both sides of the table. Even the youngest clutched a wooden platter called a trencher during Father's thanks to God, waiting to grab for a slice of bread. Most of the year Mother added a soup of carrots or cabbage or turnips from her garden. Once in a while they had bacon or milk or curds. Only rarely did they have roast or boiled beef. More often they had roast pigeon from the coop in the garden. Only rich people ate meat every day.

By a window Willy's father Edmund labored all day on a huge complicated contraption called a loom. He was a weaver. On a bench built into the loom his father sat, hands and feet in constant motion, weaving from wool threads a tough cloth called "tammy." Naturally, Willy had to know all about it.

"See at other end of the loom, Willy," said his father, "that axle with a reel of threads? Those are called the warp threads. See this axle by my shins. That rolls up the finished tammy. With my feet I make a treadle rotate both axles. With my hands I make the flying shuttle weave woof threads from these two bobbins on the sides so that they interlace with the warp threads."

"And will I weave worsted cloth someday too, Father?"

"No."

"But you are a weaver and you said Grandfather was a weaver."

"Times have changed. Men are inventing machines very rapidly now, Willy. Why, it was only a few years ago that a man named John Kay invented the flying shuttle for the loom. That made weaving with a loom much faster. Now I hear a man has invented a machine for spinning thread. The next invention, my lad, will be a machine that weaves cloth —*without the weaver.*"

"But doesn't that mean you will be without work, Father?"

"Not to worry, son. I'll soon be the new parish clerk. I can read and write very well, thanks to the village granting me one of the twelve free spaces in the parish school when I was but a boy your age. God has looked upon our family kindly."

Willy was speechless. It did seem wonderful that his father found another job if weaving was a job with no future. But somehow God did not seem close to Willy. He couldn't remember not going to the large parish church on the hill and walking down a red-carpeted aisle to sit in a pew of rich brown oak. He couldn't remember not hearing virtue extolled by the pastor in his elegant habit. He couldn't remember not seeing Christ and the Virgin in the cut-glass windows behind the altar. He couldn't remember not memorizing Bible verses, then actually reading verses after his father taught him to read. And yet, to Willy, God Almighty was invisible, remote. Maybe Father's good fortune was nothing but good luck. Was God looking out for the family when Willy fell out of a tree and lay in bed for several days? A branch snapped and he plunged to the earth. It was a good while before he could even remember his own name. Why didn't God keep the branch from breaking? Wasn't it just bad luck for Willy like the new job as parish clerk was just good luck for his father?

His father was staring at him. "Are you listening to me,

Willy? That's not all, my lad. With my new job as parish clerk go the additional duties as schoolmaster of the parish school. And that's not all either. We will be moving to the schoolhouse."

"Moving? To the schoolhouse!"

two

*T*hat very year of 1767 the five Careys moved to the schoolhouse on the hill next to the parish church. The schoolhouse was a low thatched building, much larger than their old cottage. The part used for school was not demanding on the family. Father Carey simply sat out some rough benches for the students and stood in front of a chalkboard. That's when Willy got another surprise.

"You are one of the students!" announced his father.

But with the hours of schoolwork a new freedom came to Willy too. His father was too busy with his duties as parish clerk to keep track of him as he once had. At first Willy spent his free time with boys of the village, most of whom sang in the church choir like he did. And each additional boy multiplied the group's daring tenfold. They played football in open fields, the rougher played the better. They played "staga-staga-roney," a violent game of tag. They climbed trees and leaped on unwary friends. They rang the bells of the church, relishing the moment the rope yanked them off their feet into space. They waded against the current in the river. They had staff fights by the pond, like Robin Hood and Little John, the loser hurled sprawling into the green water. They loitered around the village smithy and spit sizzlers into his fire. They cursed and scowled and yelled as he hammered on the anvil.

"Willy, my lad," said his father once at supper, his forehead creased with worry, "pray tell me you were not with those

14

boys I hear threw stones at the carriages on Watling Road today."

Willy was silent. Of course he had been with the boys. He felt guilty too. One coach had stopped, the driver leaping off and chasing them. Willy escaped by dashing into a hedgerow. It was close. Lucky for him, the driver was fat and winded. In another coach a lovely, smiling face had appeared in the window, a stone bouncing inches above her head. That made him feel very bad.

"To think of that pretty face cut and bleeding from a sharp stone that I threw," he told himself, shuddering.

Uncle Peter was more pragmatic. "If local rich people like the Marriotts were riding in such a coach and they recognized the son of the parish clerk throwing rocks at them, the parish clerk might soon be weaving again for a living."

After that Willy was more restrained in his mischief. As he learned more from his father in school he was led to reading every book he could find as long as it was not too religious. Of course he devoured books on botany and insects and birds. But he read other books as well. For his curiosity was compelling. In this way he discovered the power of books. As much as he loved his surroundings he now realized only books could now take him outside his surroundings. He did read the Bible but he read only the historical books of the Old Testament as adventure stories. And what adventure it was: Joseph and his travails, David and his fights and follies. He read *Pilgrim's Progress* as an adventure story too. He read *Robinson Crusoe*. He read about Columbus.

"No wonder Uncle Peter marvels at the sea," said Willy. "Now I understand."

He assailed his friends with facts about "tacking" and

"scudding." He spoke of starboard, buntline, grommet, stern, staysail, block, port, halyard, clewline, bow, brace, lift, leach, furl and bowline.

"Columbus was just fourteen when he first went to sea," marveled Willy.

His friends started calling him Columbus. But they didn't say it in a nice way. What did they care about the ocean? They would never see the ocean. "Let's go put a smelly old polecat in the rectory!" they cried in rebellion. Of course they didn't because they couldn't find a polecat. Willy played less and less with the boys in the afternoon. They seemed all mischief and no curiosity.

So, in the afternoons Willy often roamed far and wide and alone. It was nice to sit down in a high field on a warm breezy day and read. Oh, he had to first shinny up one of the great peely barked sycamore trees outside the school. He had to sit on a branch and study the large, lobed leaves. He had to note the zigzaggy form of the twigs. He had to break open a burry seedball and watch the tiny elongate seeds drift to the ground. But then the rolling fields and woods beckoned him from his perch. He had so many interests that every day seemed a lifetime. He might be off in the meadows collecting beetles or butterflies or the egg of a lark. He might be in nearby Whittlebury Forest collecting moths off the rough bark of oak trees or crickets from beneath rotting leaves of the forest floor. He might even be gathering the bark and leaves themselves. He might be along the Tove River collecting dragonflies and limpets. Or he might be in the moat pond between the schoolhouse and rectory, collecting tadpoles or snails or stickleback fish. Of course all birds were fair game. Many ended up chittering by his bed in well-tended cages. The area around his bed was a menagerie: cages with birds, bowls full of pond water teeming with fish and snails, bottles crawling with insects.

"Careful, Polly," he would say to his toddling sister who was drawn to creatures as he was. Soon he had a brother too: Tom, born one year after they moved into the schoolhouse. It would be a while before little Tom or Polly could do much to help. But sometimes he liked to carry them with him on a short collecting trip.

Willy gardened too. He was no longer satisfied helping mother tend vegetables that would eventually end up on the table. No, he wasn't interested in stocking soup but being the steward of all creation. He brought back seeds and young plants of every kind from the field and forest. Bur reed, water parsnip, bracken, wood sorrel, saxifrage, knapweed, moneywort, and grasses of all kinds: timothy, bent, fescue, dog's tail and hair grass. He planted them and watched them with care. If a mysterious gall hung on the side of the plant he watched that too. Who knew what hideously exciting creature would eventually crawl out of it? Some of his transplanted flora died and some lived. And he remembered it all.

"Uncle Peter tells me," was what he told Polly when she asked him how he knew the name of a plant.

And it was his uncle too who helped him study the signs of nature: delicate close-knit tracks of murderous little weasels, dainty but distinctive tracks of mice and squirrels, telling triangular groupings of rabbit tracks, the narrow line of tracks left by the determined fox. Willy tried to learn all the signs, even tufts of hair and droppings. And insects and snakes and birds left trails too.

At twelve, still digesting every nonreligious book he could

17

get his hands on, he memorized a Latin vocabulary book. Suddenly he began to understand the pastor's ritualistic Latin during the church service. Good heavens, he could read Latin! This seemed another power he had found. Who could decipher Latin besides himself and the pastor? Not his father, the schoolmaster. But aside from Willy's skill at learning another language which his father did not know enough to appreciate, his only distinction in schooling was mathematics. Numbers came easily to him. And it was not just simple mathematics but anything that was curious. Many nights in bed he pondered numbers.

"Willy," said his father one night, standing over Willy's bed, "your talking woke me up. Are you having a nightmare?"

"I was merely thinking—aloud I fear—about prime numbers."

"Prime numbers?" his father asked groggily. "Those numbers that are not evenly divisible by any other numbers except their own?"

"Yes, Father. From one to 1,000, I've discovered there are 168 prime numbers. In the next 1,000 numbers there are but 135 prime numbers. It's obvious that prime numbers became progressively more rare as the numbers grow greater in magnitude. But by what rule, Father?"

"Good night, Willy," groaned his father weakly and shuffled back to bed.

Some nights it seemed Willy did not sleep at all. He couldn't be sure, of course, wrapped in his cocoon of darkness, hearing a flutter of tiny wings, a chirp, a cheep, but it really seemed he thought about things all night long. But for what purpose?

"At twelve, my schooling ends," he said to Uncle Peter. "I

fear I'm only fit for gardening and field work."

"An honorable calling," insisted Uncle Peter. "You can work with me for a while."

Willy could tell his father Edmund wasn't pleased with gardening as his choice of a calling. But what could his father offer in its stead? He had already told Willy that weaving was a poor choice with no future. So Willy began to work in gardens and fields. He rarely saw his old friends. Still, once in a while, like a colt, he pulled at the traces. In October of 1774 he sneaked away from Paulerspury with one of his old friends to hear John Wesley preach. Willy had heard about John Wesley as long as he could remember but wasn't sure just what it was that made everyone talk about Wesley. As far as Willy knew he was just a preacher. Locals told stories about Wesley's previous visits. Back in 1769 when Wesley spoke in Northampton, there was an aurora borealis the likes of which none could recall. The sky fired streaks of orange and white and scarlet. Many a sinner came forward that night, they said. A year later Wesley came back to preach from the Book of Job: "Acquaint now thyself with him, and be at peace: thereby good shall come unto thee."

"Wesley is now seventy, but as unwrinkled as a child," said his friend as they trekked toward Towcester.

"Is that why everyone talks of Wesley?" asked Willy.

"No! It's because he doesn't preach in a church at all, but out in the fields and meadows to one and all."

"He's not in the Church of England?"

"Says he is, but there are some who say he is a Methodist too."

Willy knew very little about Dissenters. His own friends, roughnecks though they were, were all bell-ringers and members of the choir. After all, the parish school took only children of those who attended the Church of England. Dissenters like Quakers, Congregationalists, Baptists, maybe even Methodists too, had to take care of their own education.

"We're too late!" cried his friend in an open area north of Towcester. "Look, everyone is departing. Wesley is gone."

"He is still there, boys," answered a man passing by.

And they soon discovered John Wesley there, in the full habit of a pastor of the Church of England. He was short like Willy. He was very wiry, sharp-faced too, but with a tranquil expression. And yes, his face was unwrinkled and in the pink of health. Wesley and a crowd of lingerers were milling about an elm tree. Willy was very familiar with it because it was the biggest tree he had ever seen. Wesley seemed very impressed too. And that sentiment could not have stirred Willy's sympathies more.

"Pray tell, dear friends," said Wesley in a voice so strong it startled Willy until he reflected that voice usually had to carry far indeed to envelop a large crowd. "I do believe," boomed Wesley, "the Lord has given you one of his finest creations. This elm appears even larger than the one at Oxford, which I myself measured twenty-two feet around. People in Oxford claim it is the largest elm tree in England."

"Someone get a tape!" screamed a voice.

"Our tree is surely larger," yelled another.

While the crowd waited, Wesley removed his habit and carefully folded it. Underneath he wore gray knee pants and a white shirt. Someone took the habit from him and handed him a three-cornered hat and a dark blue coat with tails. By then someone had located a cloth tape measure and Wesley was as engrossed in measuring the tree as Willy would have been. Willy wanted to step forward and help, but he was trembling. Truly this John Wesley was a man who had his eyes on God but his feet on the ground. Willy heard the men around the tree say it measured twenty-eight feet in circumference. A good nine feet in diameter thought Willy, who was too shaken to volunteer the number.

"Friends, you may safely say you have the largest elm tree in England that has been carefully measured," said Wesley in that surprising crisp voice.

"Sir, how do you stay so young?" asked Willy's friend brashly.

"I rise every day at four, young friend. With rare exceptions, one hour later at five I preach, one of the healthiest exercises in the world. And I never travel less, by sea or land, than four thousand five hundred miles in a year. You must try it yourself." Smiling, he mounted a horse that was brought to him. "And now we must push on to London, good neighbors," he boomed. In seconds he and several other men dressed in dark blue coats and three-cornered hats were headed south in a canter, then a gallop.

"He's got Methodist centers all over England now," said a man in awe.

"He preaches a thousand sermons a year," sighed one man. "I heard him say so."

"Been doing it for the last thirty-five years too," said another man emphatically. "I heard him say that too."

"That's nothing," said another. "Last month he was in Gwennap and preached to thirty thousand people at one sitting! I heard one of his associates say so."

"Excuse me, good sir," said Willy boldly. "How many were here today to get God's Word from the good man?"

"Six or seven thousand, I guess," shrugged one man.

Willy's mind ran with those numbers. If these men were right, then the saintly man had preached thirty-five thousand sermons. Of course he didn't attract thirty thousand every time. The thirty thousand was probably one of his best crowds ever, his Towcester elm tree. And probably he didn't average crowds of six or seven thousand either. After all, he wasn't always so well-known as now. But suppose he averaged two thousand, then he had preached to. . .

"Seventy million!" blurted Willy.

"What was that?" asked his friend, surprised at the outburst.

Willy was too dazed to answer. What possibilities he had just realized! Seventy million. Preached to by that small man who had time for a tree. Willy would have to ponder all that for a while. Was it possible to attempt such great things for God? And still have time for a tree? But what did that have to do with him? He was going to be a gardener like Uncle Peter and enjoy God's creations to the fullest.

But the summer of 1775 changed everything.

three

W illy, what happened?" cried an alarmed nine-year-old Polly one summer afternoon in 1775. "It seems my rash is worse," he said.

"Your face and hands have been red and scaly for days," said Mother. "Lie down. Poor Willy."

Uncle Peter helped him walk inside the schoolhouse. He was slightly dazed and very tired. The truth was that his skin pained him so much during the nights he scarcely slept. He lost his appetite too. And lately he had headaches. For weeks he had fretted over it. Was it exposure to the sun? Was it a reaction to some plant poison? Was it a combination of the two? Was it like the scurvy that sailors got? Was he not eating something that he needed to eat?

"It's not scurvy," said Uncle Peter, who had sailed the oceans. Suddenly his face revealed he had remembered something. "Do you have sores in your mouth, lad?"

"Yes. This past three months."

"Then I've seen it before. Hullo, Edmund." Uncle Peter looked at Willy's father, who had just rushed inside. From the rectory where he often worked at a desk by a window he had seen the two gardeners return early. Uncle Peter continued, "I don't know what causes this condition but it won't get better. Working outside will make it worse, Edmund. It can become quite severe, affecting the brain."

Willy's father put his hand on Willy's shoulder. "Then I

must forbid you to work outside, my lad."

"But what am I to do? Weave?"

"I'll make inquiries," replied his father.

And so he did. As parish clerk Edmund Carey talked to many people. Besides that, during the school year he walked two miles to Towcester twice a week to teach girls mathematics and reading. And he occasionally visited the environs of Blisworth, Roade, Pottersbury, and Piddington. So he knew a lot of people around the area. It was only a few weeks later that he revealed his findings at supper. By that time Willy's skin was nearly its normal fair hue again.

"There's a shoemaker over in Piddington named Clarke Nichols," said Edmund. "He has such a good business, he's looking for a second apprentice."

"Shoemaker?" said Willy, with more interest than the trade deserved. He had been idle too long.

The Northampton area was known for shoemaking. Everything was there for the trade: abundant hides from the livestock in the lush pastures, friendly waterways for easy transportation, oaks for the tanning process, and lastly, tradition. The same King Charles that Cromwell had defeated in the nearby hills had earlier pummeled the ancient walls of Northampton for making shoes for Cromwell's army.

"I've been to see Clarke Nichols," continued Willy's father. "He seems a godly man. The pastor there says he is a good churchman. Mr. Nichols even has a small library, which you might profit from, Willy."

"So it's settled then?" Willy had been to Piddington a time or two in his wanderings. Eight miles distant in the general direction of Northampton was the hamlet of Piddington, smaller even than Paulerspury.

"Yes, he's agreed to take you, even though I can't pay him what I should for the seven years of training."

"I'm sure he'll find a way to even the score," said Willy cynically.

"Mister Nichols is a true craftsman who makes boots and shoes, Willy," said his father defensively. "He is not merely a cobbler who repairs boots and shoes."

"I'm sorry, Father," said Willy.

Eight miles did not exactly span the Atlantic Ocean but the family was downcast the day Willy left. Ann was now twelve, Polly, nine, and Tom, seven. Of course Willy couldn't take his menagerie, so it was entrusted to Polly. Mother blinked in disbelief as her eldest was leaving the house. Father's smile was forced, as if wondering what would happen if Willy did not make the adjustment as an apprentice.

Piddington sat on a rise with an even smaller hamlet of Hackleton below it but across a brook. The two hamlets together were about the same size as Paulerspury and seemed one village too. Of the common people like William, those who did not work the land found work in two trades: weaving and shoemaking. There were few other opportunities. After he arrived at Clarke Nichols's shop, Willy soon felt he served two masters. The other apprentice, John Warr, was three years older and had grown up in family of shoemakers. It was quickly apparent too that it would be some time before Willy ever made a shoe. He did nothing but polish and lace repaired shoes and boots—when he was not delivering the finished efforts of Nichols and John Warr. In the meantime he could only dream of someday actually making a boot.

"It's quite difficult," explained John Warr. "The shoemaker must measure his customer's foot. Then he must cut the leather just right into parts for the uppers. That all has to be stitched together. Then the heel and soles go on, not to mention the fine points like welts and stiffeners and insoles that make them fit the foot as a glove fits the hand."

One thing Willy quickly learned when he was in the shop and not making deliveries was that shoemakers who had mastered their craft had hours and hours to fill with talk. There was plenty to talk about in 1776. Everyone in England was talking about their colonial jewel, America. For years, England had boasted of one victory after another in their colonies of India and America, usually over their old enemy France. But this new trouble in America was different.

"Perhaps King George the Third," said John Warr tactfully, "being king only a few years. . ."

"Fifteen years if it's been a day!" interrupted Willy loudly. Their statements were more emphatic and charged than normal because the three rarely looked at one another as they worked.

"Still, fifteen is but a few years in the reign of a king," said John, who obviously remembered the long reign of his predecessor, George the Second. "And I'm thinking perhaps the young king is a bit too determined to assert his authority. After all, these very same Americans helped us drive the French out of Canada."

"I hear it's his prime minister, Lord North," added Clarke Nichols, "who is causing the trouble, loading down the Americans with new taxes to pay. We all hate to pay taxes."

"But what will happen if we go to war?" asked John with great concern.

"There's already fighting going on," growled Clarke Nichols angrily. "But we will make short work of the Americans."

"Really?" asked Willy with no thought of diplomacy. "Let's analyze it. My uncle Peter told me the Americans are a very feisty lot, Englishmen at one time, now perhaps less. He says they will dispute every inch of ground, which they consider theirs alone. And what is more, they consider their fight a war for liberty. Such men, says Uncle Peter, will leap into a fire or rush into a cannon's mouth. . ."

"Oh, blast all that talk of liberty," sputtered Clarke Nichols over a boot. "We have a superior military force."

"At first that will be true, I admit," said Willy, now calm and deliberate. "But what will happen if the American rebels hold out through a winter or two? Then don't they gain some advantage? Their supplies are at hand all around them. Our supplies are three thousand miles across an ocean. . ."

"Well then, the fight must be pressed to a quick finish!" insisted Clarke Nichols. "Surely our generals wouldn't be so foolish as to dawdle against the Americans."

"Well, with so many people eking out a living in England," interrupted John Warr, "I for one resent the king spending so much of our tax money on the colonies."

As hot as the talk became about America it wasn't as volatile as the two boys' arguments about religion. Only when Clark Nichols was not in the shop did the boys argue religion. Or at night up in the attic where they bunked the boys would argue. Willy considered himself a loyal churchman of the Church of England. John Warr was a Dissenter. His whole family in Pottersbury were Dissenters. His grandfather had founded an independent church there. In Piddington John Warr had joined a group of Dissenters who had been meeting since 1767. They now had a meetinghouse in Hackleton, although they had no formal church building. Large indeed at about two hundred, the group was made up of field-workers, domestic servants, and shoemakers.

"Go to the Scriptures, Willy," advised John Warr. "Decide for yourself what God says."

Willy realized he did not know much Scripture. Yet in their disputes it was usually Willy, defender of the Church of England, who seemed to win every point. But in his heart he knew he was winning only because he was more articulate than John Warr. It always seemed to him later that John Warr had won the argument. Well, he must fortify himself for such disputes. He must not win them simply because he could express himself better. That was not reasonable and Willy considered himself a very reasonable person. He made a few fumbling efforts at praying at night but at fifteen it was so much easier to think on other things.

In December he ran errands all the way into Northampton for Clarke Nichols. In the process of making purchases for the shop he also made purchases for himself. He kept the money separately. On the way back to Piddington he made the chilling discovery that among his own change was a counterfeit shilling. Worst luck! And he was so poor. Yet, there remained a way out. Why didn't he exchange the counterfeit shilling with a shilling in Clarke Nichols's change? Who would know? Surely Mister Nichols could afford such a setback better than could he, a poor apprentice boy. Not to mention Mister Nichols's waste of good money at the local tavern once a week! "Please, God, let me do this," he prayed, "just one time. I'm so poor." So when he returned he gave Mister Nichols his altered change.

"Say, lad, this shilling is counterfeit!" exploded Nichols.

"It is?" replied Willy weakly.

"You knew that, didn't you?" snapped Clarke Nichols.

Willy had no ability to lie. Was he going to shame himself further? He said, "Yes, I knew."

"You're acting so guilty I suspect the coin was in your own change before you realized it was counterfeit, then you switched it into my change. Is that not true?"

Willy took a shilling out of his own change. "Here, sir."

Willy trudged up into the attic. He lay on his cot, feeling very guilty. God had taught him a hard lesson. How could he have asked God to sanction such a dishonest thing? Suddenly Willy realized he was probably going to have to leave Piddington! Clarke Nichols would not have him as an apprentice now. Willy was going to be thrown out. He was going to lose his chance at a profession. He was going to be humiliated. John Warr would frown at him with deep disappointment. Then Willy would go home and the family would find out why he came back. They would be so ashamed of him. Polly would be heartbroken. Her big brother was a common thief. Little Tom would bawl, "My brother is a thief." Then the whole village of Paulerspury would eventually find out, the way people gossip. "Look," they would say, "it's that dirty little thief, Willy Carey. Watch your goods when he's around."

"Willy!" called Clarke Nichols from below.

"Yes, sir," he replied in terror. "I'm getting my things together," he continued weakly.

"This isn't Sunday. Get down here and get to work!"

And so Willy went back to work, at first expecting Clarke Nichols just wanted another day's work out of him. But the subject of the counterfeit shilling did not come up again that day or the next day or the next. How wrongly Willy had judged Mister Nichols. Among his numerous prayers now he

29

prayed for Clarke Nichols. And when Mister Nichols announced he was going to marry Frances Howes in October of 1777 Willy prayed for her too. He had a second chance. He was going to change his life. The theft of the coin had proven once and for all he was a sinner. And he wanted to change as John Warr had changed, for his fellow apprentice had surely become more tolerant, more loving, before Willy's very eyes.

Willy began to avidly read the Bible and books from Clark Nichols's small library. Books by Jeremy Taylor taught him how a person tries to attain a greater level of holiness in his life. Apparently this quest for personal holiness was the thrust behind John Wesley's Methodism too. For the first time Willy began to think maybe a Christian needed to do more than attend church. Maybe there was an additional obligation to search deeper. This is what the Dissenters were doing. Or were they simply rebelling against a Church of England that was controlled top to bottom by the nobility? Whatever the reason, Willy found himself enthralled in searching deeper.

"I'll fortify myself with Mr. Nichols's commentary on the New Testament," said Willy one day. "But what's this?" he asked as he tried to read parts of the commentary. "A different alphabet?"

Clarke Nichols himself could not decipher the strange alphabet. On a trip to Paulerspury Willy consulted Tom Jones, a very well-educated weaver. "Why, it's the New Testament in Greek, my lad," said Jones. "Didn't you know it was originally written in Greek?"

Greek? Willy had to think about that. When John Warr had challenged him to read the Bible, he had naturally picked up his King James Bible. He had begun to love the poetic beauty of the King James Bible. But now this. Greek!

"Do you know Greek, Mr. Jones?"

"At one time I knew some. Surely you don't think you'll master Greek, do you?"

"I learned Latin once."

"Dulce et decorum est pro Dominus laboro," said the weaver slyly.

"Yes, it is sweet and proper to work for the Lord," said Willy, hardly thinking.

The weaver looked chastened. "I'll get a glossary and a grammar for you—in Greek."

Almost effortlessly Willy learned Greek by reading the New Testament as it was actually passed on by the first church fathers. The Greek was simple street language but beautiful. Willy began to appreciate John Warr's personal struggle to understand the Scriptures. He also began to see just how much of his Church of England service had been added by later men of the church. So what was he to make these later additions? Were they added by God? Or men?

"Come with me to a meeting of Dissenters, Willy," implored John. "What is the harm? It is not a service but a discussion group."

And so Willy did attend meetings. To offset any talk about his desertion of the Church of England he attended services there three times on Sundays. He tried to keep an open mind in the Dissenter meetings. The discussions he listened to raised many questions in his mind. He listened to mystics who followed the teachings of William Law. He read. He talked with Dissenters of all sorts. They were serious Dissenters. He had never been around such searching souls as he found in Piddington. They seemed to nurture him, much as the women of nearby Bedford had nurtured the great John Bunyan in his days of doubt. Willy read all about that in Bunyan's *Grace Abounding*. There seemed little argument in the meetings over the old question of whether good works or faith or both saved a soul. Most everyone believed faith alone was enough. The real issue these days was Calvinism. Calvin's belief in predestination seemed always at the forefront of discussions.

"If we are all predestined to salvation or damnation what good is it for a person to try to do anything about it?" asked one.

"The apostles didn't mean it that way," argued another. "They only meant God knows who is saved or not saved because He knows everything. He is outside His creation and knows it from first to last. But because He knows, it doesn't mean you aren't responsible for your own salvation."

And so they argued.

The war in America was going badly. British generals had done exactly what every Englishman considered foolish. They had dawdled, as if they could finish off their weak opponent at their leisure, anytime, anywhere. And as they dawdled the Americans became stronger and the British became weaker. In 1778 France had joined the Americans. The Americans had driven the British out of Philadelphia. In dire need of divine intervention the king of England declared Sunday, February 10, 1779, as a national day for fasting and prayer.

"Come with me to the meetinghouse today, Willy," implored John Warr, "we're going to hold a service."

"But I've never gone to your service before. I only go to discussion groups."

The service seemed weak to Willy, especially because the preacher that day was Thomas Chater, a rank beginner. But after hours of prayer Chater's words built as a summer storm. Finally Chater shouted Scripture from the Book of Hebrews, " 'Let us go forth therefore unto him without the camp, bearing his reproach'!"

Willy was thrilled. His heart was on fire. Go outside the camp, bearing the disgrace Christ bore? What did that mean? Why, at that moment, it could mean only one thing. He must join these persecuted, despised Christians: the Dissenters. But could he do such a rash thing? Dissenters couldn't stand in Parliament. They couldn't send their sons to schools. They could not enter many professions. Locally they were being persecuted by Lady Elizabeth Mercer. This great owner of property evicted Dissenters from her cottages right and left. Membership in the Hackleton Meeting House was dropping.

"Yet," Willy argued with himself, "look at what these Dissenters have done for me."

In just a short time he had gained a sense of sin, the first step to salvation. He now searched and probed for the true Savior just as they did. He read the New Testament in the Greek. He was growing in holiness. And it had been through the influence of the Dissenters. Could he not stand with them in their persecution, foolish or not?

four

"**S**cripture must be the sole basis for my faith. I will be a Dissenter!" Willy told John Warr.

"And what of your family in Paulerspury?" asked Warr, happy for Willy but now concerned too.

"They won't like it. But it just adds more weight to the cross that I must carry."

It wasn't only Willy who changed. Clarke Nichols also changed. What a powerful influence the earnest John Warr was. He seemed unpersuasive at a given moment. But his truths ultimately triumphed. For Nichols truly accepted Jesus Christ as his Savior now. And what a blessing that was when just a few months later he became gravely ill. It seemed no time at all before Nichols died. He left a widow, a ten-week-old son, and his shop. Soon after the funeral the two apprentices met the widow's cousin, Thomas Old of Hackleton.

"I am a shoemaker too," he told the two apprentices. "I will be taking over the shop. We must do everything possible to ease the widow's grief."

But Thomas Old did not frequent the shop as Clarke Nichols had. As a consequence, Willy's skills as a shoemaker accelerated. It wasn't long before he was making the uppers of shoes and boots. He was nearly a complete shoemaker after five years. His competence pleased Thomas Old's wife Elizabeth, a woman in her thirties. Her father was Daniel Plackett, one of the elders in the Hackleton Meeting House.

Placketts were numerous around Piddington. It seemed every few months a Plackett baby was born in the neighborhood.

"I would like you to meet my sister, Dolly Plackett," Elizabeth Old told Willy one day.

"I've seen her often at the meetinghouse," answered Willy.

"Then you will surely want to talk to her," replied Elizabeth Old.

Elizabeth got the two together often. Dolly was a few years older than Willy. Like most young women of the parish she was unable to read or write. Willy knew few girls had been lucky like his sisters, who were educated only because their father was a schoolmaster. But Dolly conversed so brightly and cheerfully, she seized ideas so quickly, Willy never thought much about her not reading or writing. After he had seen Dolly several times it was obvious to both that they loved each other. But Willy would have to wait. Apprentices usually didn't marry.

"Fathers want a better start for their daughters than that," Willy told himself.

But that hindrance no longer applied to his friend John Warr. Now twenty-two Warr had finished his own apprenticeship. He was a shoemaker in his own right, and he married Ruth Pearson in April of 1780. He rented a cottage for his new bride. Now Willy was often in the shop alone. Without his spiritual mentor he began to drift. He didn't like the main preacher in the Hackleton Meeting House. The preacher was too much a predestinationist. So often now on Sunday, Willy walked to other churches to hear other Dissenters preach. He went to Northampton, Roade, Ravenstone—anywhere he could reach in a few hours by foot.

He even began to attend the Church of England again. In

Olney, five miles southeast of Piddington, he listened to Thomas Scott. Later, he talked to Scott. The Anglican seemed a perfect spiritual guide. Not only did he not hold to the hard predestination teachings of Calvin but he too was a gifted linguist. Willy was shocked to learn Scott had mastered Latin, Greek, and Hebrew! So, with Scott's help and books, of course Willy began learning Hebrew too.

"Now I will learn the language of the Old Testament!" he marveled.

In Towcester he listened to Thomas Skinner. Skinner was a Dissenter called a Baptist. One of the ways Baptists differed from other denominations was that they did not believe infants should be baptized. They believed only a person who could make a mature judgment should be baptized. That ordinance about baptism was the source of their name. Thomas Skinner loaned Willy a book by Robert Hall called *Help to Zion's Travellers*.

"Hall is an older Baptist pastor who lives in Arnsby, near Leicester," said Skinner.

Hall had developed arguments from verses 13 and 14 of Isaiah 57: "he that putteth his trust in me shall possess the land, and shall inherit my holy mountain; And shall say, Cast ye up, cast ye up, prepare the way, take up the stumblingblock out of the way of my people." Hall dealt with stumbling blocks to faith in Christ. But he also criticized the extreme Calvinism that paralyzed many churchmen in an attitude that God had so predestined every happening that men had few choices of their own. The book struck Willy as strongly as the sermon by Thomas Chater.

"I drank it like the sweetest wine," he enthused to Skinner. "It articulates my exact feeling for the Gospels and salvation."

Yet Willy came back to the Hackleton Meeting House too. The congregation had been his spiritual crutch for several years. He had to support it. Lady Mercer had hurt the membership. Perhaps it was time for them to fight back and become an official church. Almost in disbelief Willy found himself there to charter it with Daniel Plackett and seven other men of the congregation, including Thomas Old. May 19, 1781, the meetinghouse formally chartered itself as a Congregationalist church, which meant the local church was self-governing. The Baptists themselves were an alliance of independent congregationalist churches. But the Hackleton Meeting House did not declare itself Baptist because the members did not all agree that infants could not be baptized.

Life now seemed very stable for Willy Carey. Was the search for his spiritual ground over? Could he now forge ahead? Yes, he assured himself. Full of confidence he asked Daniel Plackett for the hand of his daughter, Dolly. And on June 10, 1781, Willy married Dolly Plackett at St. John the Baptist Church in Piddington. It was a bold move for an apprentice, possible only because Willy had many friends, not the least of which was his brother-in-law and master, Thomas Old. The cottage they rented was about as small as a cottage could be. But Dolly was ecstatic.

"Just what I always wanted, William. A loving husband and surrounded on all sides by my family. An ocean of bliss."

His parents in Paulerspury worried that he did not have the resources to support a family. But they had their own problems. Mother seemed more frail each year. Polly, now fourteen, suffered a nerve disease. Once the liveliest of girls, now parts of her body became numb. Some days she woke to find she could not move a finger or a toe. And it

37

was not getting better.

"The tender mercies of the Lord can be cruel," commented Ann, now seventeen.

In the fall of 1781 the congregation of the Hackleton church asked the apprentice shoemaker to preach a sermon. He was no longer called Willy but William, a grown man of twenty with a wife and a baby on the way. William delivered his sermon, reticent and trembling at first. Then afterward he fought the devilish warmth of pride when Dolly and members of the church praised his effort.

All Englishmen anguished a little in October of 1781. The American colonies had defeated the reticent British generals and their mercenary troops. Britain had been expelled from the colonies.

"At least we kept Canada," grumped Uncle Peter.

By the summer of 1782, William and Dolly had a baby daughter, Ann. She was sweet in looks and disposition. The Careys from Paulerspury came often to fuss over her. William and Dolly had still not come to terms with infant baptism. So baby Ann remained unbaptized. It was clear William was leaning toward the beliefs of the Baptists. And why not? Although the Anglican Scott was a major influence, most of William's spiritual mentors were Baptists, like Skinner and Hall. And as William's own reputation as a churchman spread, who most enthusiastically welcomed him? Baptists. The congregation of Baptists at Earls Barton, east of Northampton, even persuaded him to preach there every other week. It was a four-hour round trip on foot, so it was no small commitment for such a busy young married man.

One day he told Dolly, "A small group of Dissenters has asked me to lead their service once a month. And guess where? At Paulerspury!"

He did it gladly. Reports drifted to his family in Pauler-spury that he was very effective. Once he thought he saw his father Edmund at the back of the meeting. And soon Edmund even allowed him to worship with the family in their home. William burned a deck of his own playing cards in front of them. He shouted that they must be stripped of the rags of self-righteousness. At first, his parents blinked skeptically and his sisters were irritated by his evangelism. Young Tom just seemed stunned by the brother he scarcely knew.

In the winter William and baby Ann both developed fevers. Convinced it was the draftiness of the rundown cottage, they moved to another. Mother Carey came to help Dolly nurse the two sick ones. But it was too late for baby Ann. She died. William felt crushing doubt. She was not baptized. They had tested their faith with their own daughter. And if he had worked nights as a shoemaker instead of ministering at his faith, would they have had better, warmer lodgings? He certainly wasn't spending money on himself; he often trudged to meetings without a penny for a piece of bread the entire day. And he could scarcely think lately because his own fever never left except to be replaced for a while by shuddering chills. Dolly mourned for the daughter but worried about William. Would he die too? His illness continued week after week, then month after month. His hair began falling out, a symptom of the severest fever.

"You must not be fearful, Dolly," he said. "It shows you don't trust the Lord."

But something told him he had better be baptized. Yes, he had come completely around to the thinking of the Baptists. So had his two sisters, much to father Edmund's bewilderment. On the one hand Edmund was proud William was so committed and persuasive. On the other hand he was losing control of his own family, a family well supported by the Church of England. Nevertheless, both Ann and Polly were baptized in the Tove River by Thomas Skinner of Towcester in the summer of 1783. They confirmed their newfound faith even before William, who seemed to be waiting for Dolly to make the same commitment. Dolly argued that she and William both had been baptized as infants. She would not relent—unless, she hinted, William was the ordained pastor who baptized her. Finally, William would wait no longer. He was baptized on October 5 in the Nene River at Northampton by John Rylands. Rylands and his father had become spiritual advisors to William too.

"They too are Baptists," noted William of the two who pastored the College Lane Church in Northampton.

William Carey was now twenty-two, a journeyman shoemaker with an ashen, fever-sickened face and bald head. He had little energy for working. To others it seemed he had a thousand problems. To himself he was enraptured by faith. His faith was blossoming, he was sure. He was now being tested by sickness, mourning, and poverty, but no longer doubt. The winter was severe. His health and means were so obviously destitute even fifteen-year-old Tom gave him some money. Friends in Paulerspury took up a collection for the now childless William and Dolly.

"We have not suffered the most," he reminded Dolly.

Sicknesses invaded many small cottages of Piddington. Thomas Old was confined to bed. His wife Elizabeth had four children from ages three to thirteen to care for too. Then on the last day of 1783 Thomas Old died. In addition to the tragedy of losing a friend, William now had to try to salvage the business. Several clients reneged on orders. William, befuddled by fever, was bewildered by the financial end of Old's business. He had never been entrusted with that aspect of shoemaking. William found himself trudging through mud and snow, hawking for business. After all, the Widow Old and her four children depended on him now. And weren't they his very own sister-in-law and niece and three nephews? He even begged villagers for old boots and shoes so he could repair them for resale.

"If I survive this winter I can survive anything," he told himself. "Praise God for His mercy."

And praise God, William recovered his health again, if not his hair. He began tutoring students in his shop in the evenings to make extra money. His shop soon had the air of a school, with books and maps and charts always lying about. His friend Scott joked that the shop was "Carey's College." At the Hackleton Meeting House he joined discussions. Once a month now they discussed the churchman's obligation to evangelize, not just within his parish but to the entire world. Arguments flew back and forth. William found himself drawn more and more to the idea that the "Great Commission" did indeed require churchmen to spread Christ to the entire world. No longer could rigid Calvinism dismiss all efforts at missionary work in other countries as useless because God had already chosen his "elect."

"And might such an attitude just be an excuse to avoid the hard work required?" he argued.

But he was in no position to do anything but debate the proposition. All through 1784 William struggled to keep food on the table. At least by then he realized that the widow had been left enough money by Thomas Old to get by. It was time he improved the lot of Dolly. She was pregnant again. So when he heard from one of his many friends that the village of Moulton near the north edge of Northampton was losing a schoolteacher he pondered his own suitability for the job. For a long time he had belittled his own indulgences in languages and geography and botany. But friends like John Warr assured him he was a highly gifted teacher as well as a preacher.

So he sought the job in Moulton, eight miles away.

"The job is yours, Mr. Carey," he was told. "But we have no schoolhouse. You will have to provide the schoolroom yourself."

On March 25, 1785, William and Dolly moved into a cottage at the far end of Moulton. It had been a shoemaker's cottage, with a large trough near the front door for soaking leather. The experience after Thomas Old's death had soured him on the business end of shoemaking, so he arranged to make shoes and boots for a wealthy businessman in Kettering named Thomas Gotch. Gotch was a Baptist churchman, so he knew a little about William. Near the towering spire of Kettering's church was Gotch's neat three-story house of white brick. Once every two weeks William was to walk ten miles northeast of Moulton to Kettering to deliver his finished products to Gotch and pick up fresh leather and supplies. Hopefully by practicing his profession in this way, teaching school, and lay preaching here and there, he could provide for Dolly and the new baby. Baby Felix, born soon after they moved in, was not named for the dubious procurator of Judea in the Book of Acts.

"Felix is Latin for 'happiness,' " explained William, now

wise enough to cherish every moment with the child.

William was an enthusiastic teacher, although he felt the classroom of restless, chattering boys was always out of control. On one entire wall of the cottage he fashioned with sheets of paper his own world map, sketching in the countries. He added cities, populations, and religions. He even made a globe of leather, covering it too with all the countries of the world. Besides geography he taught mathematics, reading, and history. And he taught his boys that Scripture grounded all knowledge. Meanwhile outside the cottage he preached, secretly indulging the dream of being ordained someday as a Baptist minister. Imagine. Himself, William Carey, a pastor. But he was still green. Often a sermon he felt was his finest was poorly received, even by his spiritual mentors. On the other hand, a sermon he felt weak and crude might be followed by enthusiastic praise.

"I'm not quite ready," he told himself, realizing his attitude had changed from doubting his calling to patience. He joined the Baptist Church at Olney, pastored by John Sutcliffe, who now seemed most in harmony with his own thinking.

In 1785 the *Northampton Mercury* published a series of extracts from the logbook of Captain James Cook's last voyage. The exotic travels of the great English explorer to the South Seas had been talked about for years by his countrymen, long before his tragic death at the hands of Sandwich Islanders in 1779. William admired everything about James Cook except one prejudice of the notable explorer. Cook expressed the attitude of many educated English that the heathen could not be evangelized. Cook's conclusion was based on pure pragmatism:

> *. . .it can neither serve the purpose of*
> *public ambition nor private avarice; and,*
> *without such inducements, I may pro-*
> *nounce that it will never be undertaken. . .*

As much as William admired Cook, he refused to accept that cynicism. The vast sea of pagan humanity began to haunt William Carey. Just how many pagans were out there? Surely the Gospel of Christ had reached only a minority of the humans he noted on his world map. What had happened? For one thousand years after the Crucifixion, the apostles and their bold followers had fervently spread the message of Christ. Then some kind of indolence had set in. Why had the Great Commission stopped? Wouldn't it be wonderful if he, William Carey, could go to some tropical island like Tahiti and convert the heathen?

"Oh, Tahiti!" he enthused to his students, regaling them with the facts that lured him there. "Four hundred square miles of lush, green paradise. Cold weather and hot weather are unknown. Breadfruit, bananas, and coconuts hang everywhere for the eating. Bays and lagoons are choked with fat, lazy fish. And most important, lads, there are thousands of pagans! Pagans! Oh, they are most fastidious. They bathe three times a day. They are polite, yet as ignorant of the Ten Commandments as beautiful tropical birds. . ." He would go on to describe the mountains, the rivers, the bays, the coral reefs, the ease of their language. He devoured Cook's writings so avidly he felt he had been there.

That summer he was shocked when he read a treatise by Andrew Fuller, a Baptist pastor in nearby Kettering. William had heard the burly, ebullient Fuller preach in Olney. Fuller was only a few years older than William. And his treatise, titled *Gospel Worthy of All Acceptance*, could have been written by William! Fuller complained that extreme Calvinism had vanquished human responsibility toward the unchurched. Robert Hall had made that point in *Help to Zion's Travellers*. Good men could not simply sit back and assume God would select those who would get salvation. The apostles had not done that!

In the meantime the congregation of Baptists at Moulton offered him their pastorship. It was an old congregation, stretching back to the days of Oliver Cromwell the century before. But it was adrift, often not meeting at all, with a meetinghouse crumbling apart. The faltering congregation did not mind that William was not ordained. Lay preachers were allowed by the Baptists. William hesitated. Of course he could use the stipend they offered. It was about half what he earned shoemaking, and it would be most welcome. But what of his lack of experience? Was he a "novice. . .lifted up by pride" that alarmed Saint Paul? His heart in his mouth he trudged to Olney to consult one of his spiritual advisors, John Sutcliffe.

five

"*D*o I have the qualities of an elder?" William asked John Sutcliffe.

"Most assuredly, brother," answered Sutcliffe.

"Is my preaching sufficient?"

"Do it, brother," advised Sutcliffe.

So William began to rebuild the church in Moulton, not the dilapidated meetinghouse of course, but the faithful. He had much to be thankful for as 1786 bloomed. Baby Felix was healthy. Dolly was healthy. He had his own health back. His church was growing. He taught Dolly to read and write. He even had time to indulge his love of languages, knowing now he had a special gift as he learned foreign tongues with stunning quickness. His income was now sufficient. Things improved even more as influential people in the Baptist Church came to visit him. One of the first was exuberant Andrew Fuller.

"You've recently mastered Italian, French, and Dutch?" asked Fuller in disbelief.

"Yes," answered William, almost guiltily. "Brother Ryland was very upset that I did so too. His father would be even more so if he knew."

"And what of this great map on the wall?"

William explained how for each country he annotated information about population, politics, religion, and other facts. Finally he was overcome with emotion as the reality struck him once again. "Don't you see, Brother Fuller? Most of the world does not know Christ. Everywhere we look there are pagans! Pagans. Pagans. Pagans."

Andrew Fuller blinked. "Your map is indeed a powerful demonstration of that fact." His mind was churning. "I say, William, as I came in the front door did I not see leather soaking in that trough?"

"Does the smell offend you?"

"Not at all. It is only the time I envision you working on that leather that offends me."

What did Andrew Fuller mean? Was this fine man flawed? Did he see shoemaking as too insignificant? As Scripture advised, William reserved judgment, just as he had many times lately. The Rylands did not approve of some of the things he was doing either. His own father was probably disappointed in him too. But the next time William delivered his finished products to Thomas Gotch he was very glad he reserved judgment on Fuller.

"How much do you earn from me for your shoemaking, William?" asked Gotch.

William wanted to blurt, "Is my work not satisfactory?" but kept his temper. "About ten shillings a week, sir."

"Then from now on I will pay you ten shillings a week not to make shoes!"

"Not to make shoes?" asked William in amazement. "But I don't understand. . ."

Thomas Gotch smiled. "Brother Fuller was here to see me, William. He tells me you are studying foreign languages and laying groundwork for something very important for God. So you have far too much to do to make shoes."

"I praise God for your generosity, sir."

Later that year he was invited to be a member in the Northampton Baptist Association of Pastors. At the first meeting the elder Ryland moderated and insisted William Carey propose a theme for discussion. William was surprised. Should he mention his passion? His mind was made up by Scripture, Saint Paul's true words in the Second Book of Timothy: "For God hath not given us the spirit of fear; but of power, and of love, and of a sound mind."

He stood humbly. "Good sirs," he began, "perhaps we could discuss whether or not the Great Commission given the apostles in the Book of Matthew to teach all nations is not binding on all succeeding ministers to the end of the world. . ."

"Young man, sit down!" barked the elder Ryland. "If God wants to convert the heathen, He will do it without consulting you—or me!"

"But. . ."

"No buts, young man," interrupted the elder Ryland. "Good heavens, don't you realize that we would have to have a second Pentecost to break down the barrier of foreign languages?"

William wanted to protest that in his experience there was no foreign language he had not mastered in a year or two. But that would be too immodest. And the elder Ryland seemed far too rigid. Further discussion would only cause suspicion among some pastors that he, William Carey, was a heretic of some kind, or at least a rabble-rouser. So he sat down, now knowing some pastors not only did not want to hear about missionary work but were raised to anger over it.

"By holding my fire," he told Dolly later, "perhaps I proved to them my willingness to be humbled. Because they accepted me in the association."

Later that year William was at Thomas Gotch's house for an association meeting. He felt privileged to be part of such a group that included worthies like Robert Hall, Andrew Fuller, and John Ryland. He was not even ordained. He resolved to listen. The subject was not foreign missions anyway but the situation in India, which many Englishmen called "East India" to distinguish from the American Indians. Many also called it by its Indian name: Bengal. Lord Cornwallis, one of the generals who frittered away America, was governor of the East India Trade Company, which made him the virtual ruler of India. He oppressed the Indians, formally banning any native Indian from holding public office. The powerful Indian maharajahs allowed such heavy-handed treatment because the English guaranteed them local power and prosperity.

"There's a good-sized island off the southern tip of Bengal," said John Ryland, "under the control of the Dutch. Blast, I can't remember the name. . ."

Andrew Fuller smiled as if he recognized an opportunity. "Well, I believe we have in our midst a most knowledgeable man on geography. . ." He turned to look at William.

"I believe, sir, the island you speak of is Ceylon," replied William and lapsed into silence.

Andrew Fuller laughed. "Come now, William, don't hold out on us. Tell us all you know."

"If you wish, sir. Ceylon is a tropical island about half the size of England's fifty thousand square miles. And yes, it is true it is controlled by Holland." William, quickly caught up in the wonders of Ceylon, went on to describe the terrain, the monsoon season, the size of the population, and the kinds of languages spoken. After several minutes of detail his voice flamed with passion, "But in spite of Dutch control it is not a Christian country by any means. There is no more than a small percent of Christians." His voice carried indignation now, "The vast majority are Buddhists with a substantial number of Hindus." At last he cried, "Millions of poor souls lost in heathen darkness! While we do nothing!"

"But that's not true, Brother Carey," countered one of the others defensively. "We pray for the heathen. We've done so, fervently, since our resolution to do so in 1784."

And so the matter stood.

The year 1787 brought joy and woe. That summer his mother, not even fifty years old, died of a throat infection. How the Carey home in Paulerspury had changed. Only Ann and his father Edmund remained the same. Tom had already left the house, enlisting as a soldier—much to the family's consternation. "Praise God, the war in America is over," said Father. But England seemed always to be fighting France or Holland. Sister Polly still deteriorated. Now at twenty-one she could scarcely rise from bed. Ann helped care for her. But how long would Ann be there? She was now twenty-four.

"Don't you worry, Polly," Ann reassured her. "I may marry but I won't leave you."

Just weeks after his mother's funeral William was ordained a Baptist minister in the decrepit Moulton meetinghouse. In August twenty Baptist ministers were present, including Ryland and Fuller. A collection had been gathered beforehand so William would have a black suit to wear.

He believed the pastoral office "the highest honor on earth." Nothing could surpass it. And a heavy duty it was, to be teacher, bishop, and overseer of his flock. William, ever milder from his spiritual growth, did not like admonishing people, even though Scripture required it. Drunkenness, gossip, unkindness, and stinginess were just a few of the flaws he was forced to try to correct in his congregation.

One of his first duties was to consecrate Dolly into the faith. And he baptized her in October, slightly worried about the river's chill because she was pregnant again.

Meanwhile William campaigned for missionary work too. He was careful about bringing up the subject in association meetings. It was divisive. So he worked on individuals. The call to evangelize compelled him. He found more and more evidence in Scripture. Now the Book of Isaiah spoke to him more than ever before of God's desire to spread the Gospel over the entire world. In chapter 54, God said:

> *. . .more are the children of the desolate than the children of the married wife, saith the Lord. Enlarge the place of thy tent, and let them stretch forth the curtains of thine habitations: spare not, lengthen thy cords, and strengthen thy stakes; For thou shalt break forth on the right hand and on the left; and thy seed shall inherit the Gentiles. . .*

Was that not a clear call to go forth? And farther on in chapter 54 he read:

> *For thy Maker is thine husband; the Lord of hosts is his name; and thy Redeemer the Holy One of Israel; The God of the whole earth shall he be called.*

And how is Christ to be called such over the "whole earth" if the Gospel is not spread over the "whole earth"? William read more of what was required:

> *And all thy children shall be taught of the Lord; and great shall be the peace of thy children. In righteousness shalt thou be established: thou shalt be far from oppression; for thou shalt not fear: and from terror; for it shall not come near thee. . .*

"All children shall be taught of the Lord"! In chapter 55 of Isaiah, God said, "nations that knew not thee shall run unto thee because of the Lord thy God, and for the Holy One of Israel. . ." Could the obligation to explain the Gospel to others be more clear that? The Book of Isaiah was bursting with commitment! Farther on God said, "So shall my word be that goeth forth out of my mouth: it shall not return unto me void. . ." His Word must not come back void! In chapter 56 was "Neither let the son of the stranger, that hath joined himself to the Lord, speak, saying, The Lord hath utterly separated me from his people. . ." Who but a heathen could be the "stranger"? And what of the Scripture "mine house shall be called an house of prayer for all people"? Could anything be more definite than "for all people"?

William also studied the works of missionaries who had recognized the call. Of course Saint Paul was the missionary without parallel. But there were a few recent ones too. One missionary who especially appealed to him was John Eliot, called the "Apostle to the American Indians." He went to America in 1631 and learned the language of the Indians in the colony of Massachusetts. He preached the Gospel to them in their own language, then taught them to read a catechism he had written in their language. His crowning achievement was translating the Bible into their language.

"What a great thing to do for God's purpose," marveled William.

He learned John Wesley had wanted desperately to evangelize the Choctaws in America but was prevented from doing so by powerful James Oglethorpe for political reasons. This just further strengthened William's conviction that the current churches were listless and had abandoned the Great Commission. But what could one insignificant pastor in Moulton do?

In 1788 a second son was born. This one they christened William, Junior. Perhaps the boy, whom they called Willy, would not mind carrying his father's name now that William had a successful pastorate. The old vibrancy of the congregation was restored, but the same could not be done with the old meetinghouse.

"It is too dangerous to restore," William told people to whom he appealed for building funds.

That same year while appealing for funds for the new church building in Birmingham, a burgeoning manufacturing city about forty miles west of Moulton, he met a young deacon named Thomas Potts. Potts had been to the lower Mississippi Delta area around New Orleans in America. There he had dealt with American Indians. They were very receptive to new teachings, he said.

"That's most encouraging," said William. "Yes, it appears that many heathen are hungering for the Word." He then went on to tell Potts of his own compilation of foreign lands, populations, and religions.

Potts was aghast. "Good heavens, you must get a pamphlet printed with this information. I doubt anyone has done such a thing before, brother."

"I have no such time or funds. The building of the church must come first. Perhaps I could ask one of pastors of the other congregations to write such a pamphlet."

Potts smiled. "And how would they do it? No one has your knowledge. Build your church first, brother. But then if you decide to write your pamphlet, I promise you I will pay to have it printed myself!"

In early 1789, his sister Ann married William Hobson who farmed near Cottesbrooke, not far from Olney. William Carey was glad to see his family again at the wedding. Father Edmund was healthy, but Polly was paralyzed except for her right arm. They all learned Dolly expected yet another child. While there William told his whole family something that was weighing on his mind. He had been offered the pastorate at the Harvey Lane meetinghouse in Leicester. Distinguished once, the congregation now was in disarray, much as Moulton had been. But Leicester was a good-sized town, with 17,000 people living there. Potentially the pastorage there was much larger than one could ever be in a village like Moulton. Wealthy noblemen were at that very moment building a canal to Leicester that would open the town up even more to trade. What should he do?

"The people at Leicester need your help," volunteered Ann. "You've rejuvenated Moulton. Can't you leave it in good hands?"

So William began to rehabilitate another congregation. Leicester was sixty strong when he arrived, but they looked very few in the large whitewashed meetinghouse that could hold up to three hundred. The three-story brick rectory stood directly across Harvey Lane from the meetinghouse. In a study on the third floor William looked out a dormer onto his church. His family now numbered five, with the addition of a third son, Peter. Beyond the cottage, green fields and gardens sloped down to the Soar River. As always William and Dolly managed a superb garden. His stipend was not enough though. Once again he taught school. Once again his schedule was crushing. He wrote his father of his duties beyond teaching school:

> *On Monday I confine myself to the study of the learned languages, and oblige myself to translate something. On Tuesday to the study of science, history, composition, etc. On Wednesday I preach a lecture and have been more than a year on the Book of Revelation. On Thursday I visit my friends. Friday and Saturday are spent in preparing for the Lord's Day, and Lord's Day preaching the Word of God. . .I have acted for twelve months as Secretary to the Committee of Dissenters. . .Add to this occasional journeys, ministers' meetings, etc. and you will rather wonder that I have any time (left). . .[1]*

If this new pastorage was not demanding enough, for the first time he ran into members of the flock who fought every move to improvement. No wonder three pastors had resigned in three years. It seemed he tended a flock of devils at times.

The birth and death of a daughter, Lucy, made the ordeal even worse. Lucy's tender innocence reminded William he could fail too. Would he at last fail a congregation? Even venerable old Robert Hall of Arnsby couldn't influence the flock. In fact, with brutal frankness, he shook William's confidence even more by criticizing his sermons.

"Your sermons have no 'likes' in them, brother. You give your flock no applications to everyday living."

And at one association meeting at Clipston, William again tried to stir consciences over the heathen. Impulsively he stood at their evening dinner and quoted Saint Paul from the Book of Romans:

> *How then shall they call on him in*
> *whom they have not believed? and how*
> *shall they believe in him of whom they have*
> *not heard? and how shall they hear without*
> *a preacher? And how shall they preach,*
> *except they be sent? as it is written, How*
> *beautiful are the feet of them that preach*
> *the gospel of peace, and bring glad tidings*
> *of good things!*

"Oh, for heaven's sakes, Brother Carey, the age of apostles is over," one anguished voice cried out in reply. Others squirmed in silence.

And yet out of this turmoil William grew as a rose in a thistle patch in Leicester. He had an intellectual life he had never known before. His friendships were numerous. He was told he "spoke well on almost everything" by men as diverse as Robert Phillips, a radical journalist, and Robert Brewin, a botanist, and Thomas Arnold, a physician doing pioneer work in mental illness. They loaned him books. A library at Guild Hall loaned him books too. And despite his crushing work schedule he crafted the "pamphlet" urged by Thomas Potts. After three years, even the evil in his congregation seemed to at last die. His church began to grow.

"God's hand is on this," marveled William. "I pray He is using me as His instrument."

The "pamphlet" urged by Thomas Potts he now titled *An Enquiry into the Obligations of Christians to Use Means for the Conversion of the Heathens, in Which the Religious State of the Different Nations of the World, the Success of Former Undertakings, and the Practicability of Further Undertakings are Considered.* The title surely told anyone the publication would not be a pamphlet. It turned out to be an eighty-seven-page book.

In the first section William asked the key question: Is the Great Commission still binding? And in this section he reviewed every objection he had ever heard against missionary work. Then he rebutted it. Examples of these were:

> Objection: But how do we know that this command is still valid? Not even divine injunctions abide forever. They have their periods and pass, like the Levitical law.
>
> Reply: Nay, divine injunctions abide till they have fulfilled their function. Who can think this commission exhausted, with the majority of mankind not yet acquainted with Christ's name?
>
> Objection: But Christ's command could scarcely

have been absolute, even for the apostles, seeing that they never heard of vast parts of the globe—the South Seas for example —nor could these be reached. Neither can we think it absolute today, with very large regions still unknown and unopened.

Reply: As they (the apostles) were responsible for going according to their strength into all their accessible world, we are in duty bound to speed into our much enlarged world. Indeed, we ought to be keen to go everywhere for Christ, till all closed doors are opened.[2]

In the second section William took the history of missionary work from the apostles to the most recent efforts of the Danes in India. The names were illustrious: Saint Paul, the apostle Thomas to India and China, Columba to Scotland, Patrick to Ireland. And the fact that Catholics, German Moravians, the Dutch and the Danes were actively establishing missions all over the world at the very moment the English Protestants procrastinated seemed a stinging rebuke!

In the third section William laid out in tables the information he had long compiled on his great wall map of the world: each country, its size, its population, its religions. He had information down to the details of a Swiss canton or one island of the seven Sandwich islands. His conclusions were staggering to those complacent souls who considered themselves safely ensconced in a Christian world:

The inhabitants of the world, according to this

*calculation, amount to about 731 millions: 420 mil-
lions of whom are still in pagan darkness; 130 millions the followers of Mahomet; 100 millions
Catholics; 44 millions Protestants; 30 millions of
the Greek and Armenian (Orthodox Christian)
churches, and perhaps 7 millions of Jews. It must
undoubtedly strike every considerate mind what a
vast proportion of the sons of Adam there are who
yet remain in the most deplorable state of heathen
darkness, without any means of knowing the true
God. . .and utterly destitute of the knowledge of the
Gospel of Christ. . .* [3]

So 76 percent of mankind did not know the Gospel! Or 557
million souls! Who but a fool could be complacent? William
couldn't resist adding that many of the pagan countries prac-
ticed abominations like cannibalism and human sacrifice.
That was not rumor, but fact reported by stalwarts like James
Cook who were not sympathetic to missionary goals.

The fourth section of the book was pragmatic, discussing
the practicality of undertaking missionary work in such far-
off foreign countries. Far distances and language barriers
never stopped traders, he argued. Who could deny that? So
the missionary must not be stopped either. Hunger would
rarely be an obstacle, insisted William. The missionary could
farm, fish, and hunt. But nevertheless the missionary must be
resolved to face poverty, poor housing, and unrelenting hard
work. And yes, he may also face hatred, intimidation, imprisonment, torture, and even death.

His last section outlined what he thought was the duty of
the "average" Christian. Every Christian must *pray*. God will

answer. And besides praying, Christians must *plod* and *plan*. Local missionary societies must be formed in each denomination, and yet they should make every effort to commune with each other. The societies must deliberate on where and when the commission will be attempted. Then stout hearts must volunteer to do the mission work. Probably an ideal team at first would be two married men; their families might come later. Then all the Christians in the congregation must fund them. The congregation must support the missionaries with money and supplies.

He ended his eighty-seven pages with a rousing rally cry:

> *What a heaven to see the myriads of the heathen,*
> *of Britons among the rest, who by their labors have*
> *been brought into the knowledge of God! Surely*
> *such a crown of rejoicing deserves our aspiration!*
> *Surely it is worthwhile to lay ourselves out with all*
> *our might in promoting Christ's kingdom!*[4]

By May 12, 1792, the *Enquiry* was printed and advertised in the *Leicester Herald.* Just a couple of weeks later black-garbed ministers of the twenty-four churches in the Northampton Baptist Association would meet at "The Angel," an inn in Nottingham, twenty miles north of Leicester. There William intended to press his cause openly. Would it once again be met by failure? Only God knew.

six

When the ministers of the Northampton Baptist Association first convened on the evening of May 30, 1792, they mourned the loss of fiery old Robert Hall. Then they gave their local reports. Several congregations still fought dissension or listlessness. But the news was not all bad. Congregations at Nottingham, Kettering, Guilsborough, Walgrave, Clipston, Gretton, Roade, Arnsby, Bottesford, and Foxton were on the upswing. And William, most grateful to God, was able to report Harvey Lane had at long last healed its dissensions.

William also mentioned his *Enquiry* was available. "For those who want it," he added hopefully.

The ministers spoke awhile of France. The revolution that started in 1789 was still simmering. King Louis XVI gave the people some rights but stayed in power. As recently as April he created a diversion by attacking the Germans. But if the king failed, speculated the ministers, could he last? And who would rise in his place? Some in England were saying that if the revolutionaries were successful, they would kill the entire French aristocracy. And what would be the result for England?

Next morning at ten o'clock William had a unique opportunity. For it was he who would deliver the sermon for the meeting. And to the discomfort of many there he preached on Isaiah 54. " 'Enlarge the place of thy tent, and let them stretch forth the curtains of thine habitations: spare not, lengthen thy cords, and strengthen thy stakes'!" he exhorted his fellow ministers. Once again he had delivered his message of obligation to convert the heathen.

Finally he concluded, "Brothers, expect great things from God. Attempt great things for God."

Young John Ryland looked shaken. "Brother Carey, I think you have proved our negligence in this cause of God."

Bringing John Ryland to the cause was a great step forward. William knew he already had one powerful ally in Andrew Fuller. But at the business meeting later, not only was no money allocated toward a missionary society but not one minister seconded William's motion to form a society. William slumped in his chair, his mind reeling.

"This meeting is adjourned, brothers," announced Andrew Fuller, who chaired the meeting.

William leaped to his feet. "Is nothing going to be done again, sir?" he shouted at Fuller. He faced the ministers. "You are like Moses' scouts who came back to Kadesh to say, 'We saw the giants, the sons of Anak, which come of the giants: and we were in our own sight as grasshoppers. . .'"

"But they lied," protested one of the ministers.

"Perhaps not. Perhaps they allowed their own minds, their own fears, their own doubts, to trick them."

Andrew Fuller seemed shaken. "I move to reopen for business."

"I second the motion," said William.

"All in favor, raise their hands," said Fuller as he glared at the other ministers.

A majority raised their hands!

Now events transpired as golden as they were ashen only

moments before. Fuller pushed, pushed, pushed, as fiery as an avenging angel. Within minutes the association had passed the following resolution:

> *Resolved, that a plan be prepared against the next ministers' meeting at Kettering, for forming a Baptist Society for propagating the Gospel among the Heathens.*[1]

"Praise God, the door is at last open," sighed grateful William.

On October 2 of that year the ministers of the association met again—this time in Kettering. As William feared, many who had been persuaded by Fuller's righteous fury at Nottingham had backed off again.

"Good heavens," confided one to William, "how can I commend such a thing to my congregation? We are so poor. It's preposterous to be thinking of foreign missions!"

His criticism is heartfelt, thought William. Sometimes he faltered himself. The reception of the rest of the English Protestants to their move to start a missionary society was proof enough. Presbyterians denounced them. Anglicans ignored them as if they didn't exist. And so did Congregationalists and many other Dissenters. But the most stunning response of all came from his own Baptists. All five of the five Baptist associations other than the Northampton Baptist Association shunned them too!

"So here we stand," reflected William, "a small association of two dozen Baptist congregations in the Midlands of England. Some of our churches are in hamlets so small a person in London would never have heard of them: Thrapston,

Cottesbrooke, Braybrooke." Several of the congregations had fewer than twenty-five members. William was all too familiar with compiling numbers. The Northampton Baptist Association represented no more than a couple of thousand Englishmen, many dirt-poor. And what was their objective? Over 500 million heathen!

"God, forgive me for such black thoughts," William finally reprimanded himself. "With God, anything is possible."

That October, twelve of the ministers finally committed their congregations to the society they defined in a resolution:

> *Humbly desirous of making an effort for the propagation of the Gospel amongst the Heathen, according to the recommendations of Carey's* Enquiry, *we unanimously resolve to act in Society together for this purpose; and, as in the divided state of Christendom each denomination, by exerting itself separately, seems likeliest to accomplish the great end, we name this the Particular Baptist Society for the Propagation of the Gospel amongst the Heathen.*[2]

In Fuller's empty snuffbox they collected thirteen English pounds to launch the society. William put in one pound from his sales of the *Enquiry*. Officers of the new society were Andrew Fuller of Kettering, John Ryland of Northampton, John Sutcliffe of Olney, Reynold Hogg of Thrapston, and William. They agreed to meet once a month.

Over the following weeks William was heartened by the twelve ministers. They were few but enthusiastic. A letter from Polly told William that his father Edmund had heard of the mission society and was very worried that William himself would volunteer to be a missionary. William wrote his father that he was at the Lord's disposal but had little expectation of actually going to a foreign country himself. Most intriguing was a letter William received from a Dr. John Thomas in London. It seemed Baptist friends there had told this physician about their new society. And Thomas was volunteering to be their missionary to India!

"He is willing to go as soon as possible," William told Dolly. "He says in his letter he has already been to India. He claims to have evangelized there already. Andrew Fuller has agreed to do some investigating in London. If Dr. Thomas seems a satisfactory fellow, then we'll have him at our January meeting in Kettering."

"And make him your first volunteer?" gasped Dolly, noting the intensity in William's eyes. "If it all works out you would like to go with him too, wouldn't you?"

"Well, I. . ."

"I won't go with you."

"But. . ."

"I'm pregnant again."

"Splendid, dear. God has blessed us again."

But later William was numb. He hadn't expected Dolly to be so firmly opposed. Of course they had discussed such a possibility. She had been silent but seemed compliant. But that was when William talked of a tropical paradise: Tahiti. And that was when the Baptist association still repelled William's ideas.

"So perhaps she held her tongue because she thought it would all come to nothing anyway," sighed William.

It was many days later when Andrew Fuller visited William

in Leicester. Fuller had indeed been in London talking to people who knew Dr. Thomas, especially Abraham Booth, a pastor who had corresponded regularly with Thomas while he was in India. Fuller had even seen Thomas himself.

"He's an exuberant gentleman to be sure," said Fuller. "Full of enthusiasm for the Gospel."

"And what about his Indian work, Brother Fuller?"

"Charles Grant, an official of the East India Company in Calcutta, arranged it. Apparently this Grant had written London clerics in the past to plead for missionaries. He got no response. So he did the next best thing. He found his own missionary among the English in Calcutta. And that missionary was Dr. John Thomas."

"And what kind of work has Thomas actually done?"

"He was sent to Malda, a village far north of Calcutta. Malda is an outpost of a few enterprising Englishmen running indigo plants."

"Making the blue dye?"

"Yes. But Thomas doctored the Indians there."

"Admirable."

"For five years."

"You don't say!"

"He learned Bengali," said Andrew Fuller with a knowing look in his eye.

"The native language? You don't say!"

"He claims to have translated the books of Matthew, Mark, and James into Bengali for the Indians."

"Translated the Bible!" William's head was spinning. Why this Dr. Thomas had done everything he wanted to do himself! Among the heathen! Translating the Word into their language! He was amazed. He scarcely acknowledged Fuller's other comments about Dr. Thomas.

"I've invited Dr. Thomas to our meeting in January, brother," concluded Andrew Fuller.

"Most appropriate," replied William, still dazed.

Only later did he ruminate on what else Fuller had told him about Thomas. Thomas was perhaps closer to Andrew Fuller's age of thirty-eight than William's age of thirty-one. He was from Gloucester, a river port on England's west coast. His father was a deacon in the Church of England. Dr. Thomas was licensed to practice medicine from his medical study in London. He had sailed to India as a ship's doctor more than once. He knew many influential Englishmen in Calcutta, the headquarters for British rule of India. His wife and daughter lived in London.

"A most interesting fellow to be sure," concluded William. "He seems too accomplished to be true."

Cold December days crawled by as William waited for the January meeting. *How quickly God had thrust the door open,* he thought. It had only been a couple of months since the Nottingham meeting when the association adjourned with no action on his motion to start a mission society. Then miraculously Andrew Fuller had come to life under William's righteous outburst.

The Bible was so wise. William had always followed the proverbs to control his anger. If it had not been so highly unusual for William to show anger his outburst would have meant nothing to Andrew Fuller. But Fuller knew William's rage came from his very soul.

On Wednesday, January 9, 1793, the Particular Baptist Society for the Propagation of the Gospel amongst the Heathen met in Kettering. William preached the sermon on the last chapter of the Book of Revelation. He had long wrestled with Revelation because many opponents of work among heathens had used it to "prove" missionary work could not begin until signs prophesied in Revelation were seen. But this day William expanded on the glorious promise of Christ: "Behold, I come quickly; and my reward is with me, to give every man according as his work shall be."

Then Dr. John Thomas arrived, limping, but his lean sharp-featured face aglow with good cheer. "Pardon me, brothers, for my tardiness. But I've injured my foot."

"Pray, come forward, Doctor," urged Andrew Fuller. "The brothers have many questions."

"What a privilege to address such a group of enthusiasts," began Dr. Thomas. "In London the people are timid, not knowing whether to applaud my efforts with the heathen or condemn me."

The physician quickly won over the brothers at the meeting. There was no doubt he knew India. He knew it as an adventurer, a doctor, and an evangelist. And there was no doubt that his attitude toward his fellowmen was perfect. He doctored everyone who came to him. He respected his charges enough to learn their language of Bengali with the help of a pundit or teacher.

"Here I have a plea from two educated Indians of the Brahmin caste, brothers," concluded Dr. Thomas, waving a letter. "They plead for your compassion. They plead for scholars who can help them translate the Word."

Translate the Word! William almost jumped out of his chair. With a few esoteric questions about linguistics William proved to himself beyond any doubt the doctor had indeed translated part of the Gospel into Bengali!

Andrew Fuller said cautiously, "Dr. Thomas, we have the thought that missionaries should be supported only through their passage to the heathen country and the first few weeks thereafter. Do you purport that missionaries can support themselves in India?"

"I do, sir. Although at first it will be a struggle."

"Would you then agree to become our first missionary?"

"Of course, brothers," he replied energetically. "That is exactly why I'm here."

So the way was clear. William could not contain himself any longer. "Brothers, I offer my own services as Dr. Thomas's assistant!"

"The society's chief linguist and planner?" Dr. Thomas beamed. "Why, I never expected such generosity!" He threw his arms around William.

Dr. Thomas recommended they sail to India in April and added cheerily that this time he wished to have his wife and daughter Betsy with him. Dazed, William nodded agreement to the April departure and trudged back to Leicester, thinking of little else but Dolly and his children. Felix was now seven; Willy, four; and Peter, three. And one child was in the womb. After Dolly's outburst, he no longer assumed she would go with him. She would probably stay. Perhaps it was best—for a period of time. After all, he had proposed that very precaution in his *Enquiry.*

"I feel guilty," he told himself. "Yet, scripturally I'm sinless. If I were not, I would not go." And as he walked along the rutted road he kept repeating verses from chapter 14 of the Book of Luke:

If any man come to me, and hate not his father,

*and mother, and wife, and children, and brethren,
and sisters, yea, and his own life also, he cannot be
my disciple. And whosoever doth not bear his cross,
and come after me, cannot be my disciple.*

When he told Dolly that he was going in April he saw fear in her face he had never seen before. She was speechless. This fork in the road was too much for her. She was crushed under William's cross. There seemed no solution to her dilemma. She dreaded going to India. She hated to leave her family. She was terrified of having a baby aboard ship. And yet if she stayed, she was sure she was a virtual widow at thirty-six. William knew all that.

"Let's think of your options, dear," comforted William. "I know this is sudden."

"I'm going!" shouted Felix.

"No!" protested Dolly. "See how you've filled his head with exotic heathen, William. He will never be happy in a hamlet like Hackleton."

"Hackleton?"

"Of course. I'll move back to Hackleton and live with my family. Kitty is still at home, unmarried. She can help me with the children and the baby."

"Why not bring Kitty with you to India?"

"I couldn't ask her to do that," replied Dolly, but a slight flicker of hope on her face revealed she suspected her sister Kitty just might go to India.

"We'll ask her."

"I can't believe you've done this to me," said Dolly, suddenly sobbing.

That Sunday William's congregation didn't accept it any

more easily than Dolly had. They were angry, confused, betrayed. "How could you?" one cried, "what about us?" William could see his years of healing the brethren evaporating as old grievances surfaced. He wrote two letters: one to Andrew Fuller, begging him to come to Leicester to soothe Dolly and the congregation, and one to his father:

> . . .*now I am appointed to go to Bengal in the East Indies, a missionary to the Hindus. . .the most mild and inoffensive people in the world; but. . . enveloped in the greatest superstition and in the grossest ignorance.*
>
> *My wife and family will stay behind at present, and will have sufficient support in my absence; or should they choose to follow me, their expenses will be borne. We are to leave England on the 3rd April next. I hope, dear father, you may be enabled to surrender me up to the Lord for the most arduous, honorable and important work that ever any of the sons of men were called on to engage in. I have many sacrifices to make. I must part with a beloved family, a number of most affectionate friends. Never did I see such sorrow manifested as reigned through our place of worship Sunday. But I have set my hand to the plough.*[3]

Polly wrote William that upon reading the letter his father Edmund had screamed, "Your brother William has gone mad!" William was not surprised. His father had always suffered great anxiety. He worried about every eventuality and when one out of ten of his worries came true, he moaned,

"You see now, don't you?" And one would never know from Polly's perky letters, reflected William, that she was now bedridden, a mute with the use of only one arm.

"Praise God for such a sister," said William, "my most faithful correspondent."

Andrew Fuller brought John Sutcliffe of Olney with him to Leicester. Their meeting with the seventy members of William's congregation was more successful than their meeting with Dolly. She would not admit to any fear of her own safety but reminded them how fragile William was. Could they not remember his struggle against fever for over a year that cost him his hair, if not his life? Did they not know India had heat and disease that no Englishman as weak as William could endure?

"I will never follow him to India," she moaned, "because he will die there!"

William journeyed many miles to raise support for the mission from Baptist brethren outside the association. On his trip north to Yorkshire he saw his brother Tom. Tom had been wounded in military service against Holland but seemed to be recovering. He had a good wife and two sons, Peter and Eustace. Always good-hearted, he was once again grounded in Christ.

Other journeys were not so pleasant for William. "Donating money to such an ill-fated mission is sinful," snapped one churchman.

For the next weeks William thought about little but India. The brothers of the mission society even paid him a stipend so he would no longer have to teach school. Although during the meeting some of the brothers of their society had sat in fear and trembling, now they threw all their energy into making the effort succeed. Soon William devoted every moment to preparation. This first effort was so important. When he asked Dr. Thomas for a grammar book on Bengali, Thomas only smiled. "We'll drill each other while aboard ship, Brother Carey, during the five long months of our journey." Five months! So William sought other facts. He learned much about the flora of India from his friend Robert Brewin. He tried to read about the Hindu religion. It seemed so hopelessly complex he went to an old professor in Leicester who did comparative studies of religions.

"What do you know of the Hindus?" William asked the professor.

"I lived in India for awhile," replied the professor, obviously pleased at William's interest. "The behavior of Hindus is far simpler than their beliefs. How could simple peasants learn such a complex system as you probably read about? If you watch them carelessly like most Englishmen you will see only that they don't eat meat, especially their sacred cows. You will see they make sure they do nothing to leave their own caste. And they make sure they marry within their own caste."

"I read in one book there are four castes. Yet in another book. . ."

The professor smiled indulgently. "The castes have been subdivided and subdivided until now there are thousands of castes."

"Thousands?"

"Their caste system is outrageous to our eyes. They believe in reincarnation. They also believe a Hindu can be reborn into a higher caste—but only if he stays strictly within his caste in this lifetime. So you see the Hindus are quite captive

73

within their caste."

"I see."

"If you really try to know the Hindus you will observe that all castes have several very formal ceremonies. Three are most important. Twelve days after birth the baby is placed in a swinging cot above twelve candles and the priest announces his name. The second ceremony is marriage, which has usually been arranged by the parents. However if a man becomes wealthy he may add wives of his own choice, and as many as he can afford! The last ceremony is for death. The Hindus believe the soul, trapped in the skull, can only be released by sacred fire. So they burn the dead. They make sure the skull is burned up or is broken open. Three days later they scatter the ashes into a river. . ."

"Why do you hesitate, sir?"

"The Hindus practice other traditions that will chill your blood. I will not speak of them. You'll learn of them if you are observant. Besides, it has been many years since I lived in India. Perhaps we English no longer allow such barbarity."

What could he mean? William thanked the professor and excused himself. He solicited others for a more recent history of the East India Company, that arm of the British Crown that really ruled India now. More aspects of going to India disturbed him. One helpful friend showed him a statute passed by Parliament:

> *Be it further enacted that if any subject or subjects of His Majesty not being lawfully licensed or authorized shall at anytime directly or indirectly go, sail or repair to, or be found in the East Indies . . .all and every such persons are hereby declared*

*to be guilty of a high crime and misdemeanor, and
being convicted thereof, shall be liable to fine or
imprisonment or both as the Court shall think fit.*[4]

"What about this 'license' that is required?" William later
asked Andrew Fuller.

"Dr. Thomas says not to worry," replied Fuller uncomfortably.

"But we are getting licenses, aren't we?"

"Apparently Dr. Thomas went to Charles Grant in London,"
continued Andrew Fuller, uncharacteristically subdued.
"Grant is now one of the directors of the East India Company.
Thomas was refused licenses. Apparently the government is
no longer indifferent to missionaries but hostile. . ."

"Hostile!"

seven

A ndrew Fuller swallowed hard and continued, "Dr. Thomas says not getting licenses is not a problem."

"And what about France?" asked a shaken William, who had heard the revolutionaries had finally tired of Louis XVI's military defeats against Germany and executed their king.

Fuller raised an eyebrow. "Who knows what the revolutionaries will do?"

"But I've heard they declared war on England. Will they attack English ships?"

Fuller laughed weakly. "They declared war on every monarch on the globe." His face darkened. "The sad truth is that they are killing all their old authorities, including priests."

"But are they no threat to our ship?" asked William hopefully.

"You will have a convoy of warships, Brother Carey. Don't forget you will be sailing on an official vessel of the East India Company, which is now run by the Crown."

At long last the time to leave approached. Dolly had resigned herself to William's mission. She even relented to let Felix go with him. The two planned to return to England in three or four years. The last days were full of tearful gatherings in Leicester. William would never have to doubt his brethren were fully behind him. Fourteen ministers came to bless his journey. The mission society had collected hundreds of English pounds, inside the association and outside. The mission would not lack for money or prayers.

William accompanied his wife and family to Hackleton in a wagon full of belongings. Then on March 26, 1793, William and Felix departed Hackleton.

"Good-bye, dear," said William calmly. "Do not fear for us. Trust God." But he saw she was terrified.

In London they made one last effort to obtain licenses. Dr. John Thomas certainly knew powerful individuals. Through Thomas, William met John Newton, nearly seventy, a well-known Anglican churchman once from Olney. Newton had been a slave runner, his soul redeemed during a violent storm at sea. About God's saving grace he had written a poem, later set to music and sung widely as a hymn. William knew it well:

> *Amazing grace—how sweet the sound*
> *   —that saved a wretch like me!*
> *I once was lost but now am found,*
> *   was blind but now I see.*
>
> *'Twas grace that taught my heart to fear,*
> *   and grace my fears relieved;*
> *how precious did that grace appear*
> *   the hour I first believed!*
>
> *Through many dangers, toils, and snares*
> *   I have already come;*
> *'tis grace hath brought me safe thus far,*
> *   and grace will lead me home.*

> *The Lord has promised good to me;*
> *His word my hope secures;*
> *He will my shield and portion be*
> *as long as life endures.*

The hymn was called "Amazing Grace."

After being introduced to John Newton, William had a momentary lapse of confidence in his mission. "But what if we are turned back because we have no licenses?" he asked Newton.

The crusty Newton seemed surprised at the timidity in the question. "Why, conclude that your Lord has nothing for you to accomplish there." He gave William a stern look. "But if He has something there for you to do, no power on earth can stop you!" He quickly dismissed William's worry. "Say, I know you good men surely must oppose the abomination of slavery. I want you to meet the man who will champion its abolition to a conclusion."

So Newton in turn introduced the two travelers to William Wilberforce. Wilberforce, about the same age as William, was said to be a force in the House of Commons, constantly haranguing the evils of slavery. He was a thoroughly good man who also thought it was high time England stopped persecuting Catholics too. William learned that Wilberforce was part of a London circle of evangelical intellectuals called the "Clapham Sect" because they all lived in Clapham, a new area of fine homes south of London. Mansions there were built in a revived Classical style with columns. The group of wealthy evangelicals also included Charles Grant and Sir John Shore, another longtime official in the East India Company. These men seemed sympathetic to converting heathens, yet now remained subdued about missionary work in India. William heard rumors in London that many influential people did not want to jeopardize their commercial interests in India by allowing evangelists to rile the natives. So William concluded the political climate was not right yet.

Such a conclusion hardly eased his worry. "And still we have no licenses?" he asked Thomas.

"We have licenses now for my wife, my daughter Betsy, your son Felix, and my two cousins, Samuel and Sarah Powell. It's not a problem." Dr. Thomas winked. "Ask Reverend John Newton."

Soon all seven were aboard the *Earl of Oxford,* a ship Thomas had served on as ship's surgeon twice in years past. He knew the captain. So William found himself with 250 other passengers in the world of seamen, a world that thrilled him as a boy. Thomas was comfortable in that world too, speaking as easily of old caravels with broad bows and narrow poop decks as of modern, swift "Baltimore clippers." William was quite impressed.

"And what kind of escort will we get?" he asked Thomas as they waited for their convoy at the Isle of Wight.

Thomas had more than enough time for erudite answers about how warships varied from "great ships" with two or three tiers of cannons to smaller, lesser-gunned ships like frigates, sloops, brigantines, schooners, cutters, and luggers. The *Earl of Oxford* waited day after day for its convoy. The delay was so long the passengers went ashore to lodge in Ryde. William wrote Dolly a letter from Ryde. He was still there when her return letter came from Hackleton.

"Felix! You are blessed with a new brother," he exclaimed. "Mother has named him Jabez."

"Jabez?" repeated Felix, puzzled.

"A fine biblical name," answered William. He didn't quote the passage in the fourth chapter of the Book of First Chronicles: "and his mother called his name Jabez, saying, Because I bare him with sorrow." Why let Felix know how unhappy his mother was?

Finally, one day in early May the captain summoned Dr. Thomas to come immediately. Thomas returned to William, for once shaken. "It seems someone has warned the captain that the authorities in Calcutta have been put on notice there is one passenger aboard without a license."

"One?" asked William in surprise.

"Yes, and that one is me, no doubt. Well, I must confess our betrayer might be one of my old debtors. You see, Brother Carey, before I sailed to India in 1786 I had mounted a considerable debt. I fully intended to pay it all back when I returned this last time from India. I had brought back oriental goods to sell in London. But I fell short, unfortunately. One of those I could not pay back apparently is bent on revenge." Thomas looked sheepish. "If I can't get it straightened out very soon the captain will put the two of us off the ship."

"Off the ship! What can we do?"

"I'll rush to London and see if I can see who is doing this to me. Perhaps I can set it right."

"I'll pray, brother."

And so Dr. Thomas made a hurried trip to London as the passengers of *Earl of Oxford* awaited their convoy in Ryde. While waiting, William learned more and more about Dr. Thomas's debts. They were massive. And it seemed everywhere he went he had such problems. India or London, it didn't matter. William grew more and more depressed. It seemed inconceivable that they would be put off the ship. After so many years of effort. After so much travail. How could it be? And what promise did his future hold with Dr. John Thomas anyway? The man now seemed a bungler of the highest order.

One day Felix was excited. "Father, look in the harbor. The warship has arrived!"

The convoy of the *Earl of Oxford!* And Dr. Thomas was not back from London. What should William do? Should he take all their goods off the ship? They had loaded goods to sell in Calcutta to finance their very difficult first year or so. Should he allow Mrs. Thomas and the others to sail? It was too much for William. He had to find a private place to shed his tears of bitter disappointment. So it had all come to this.

"Father, where are you?" called Felix. "Dr. Thomas is coming!"

"I'm sorry, brother," was all Thomas had to say when he approached William.

"We are still to be cast out then?" murmured William.

Thomas perked up. "Oh, we will get there by and by, brother."

Thomas's words were not empty because he said farewell to his wife and daughter and cousins. He was leaving them on the ship! Soon William, Felix, and the doctor watched the *Earl of Oxford* raise it sails and sail off to the south. They set off for London. William had never felt so glum. He was not such a fool he didn't know it was almost too late in the spring to sail to India. It took weeks just to get to the southern tip of Africa, then the ship had to round the cape and head northeast to India. This time of year the ship scudded across the vast Indian Ocean with ease behind the southwest monsoons.

But in the fall the winds reversed and a ship had to tack back and forth against head winds. During the winter months a ship could not get to India at all! The thought of not sailing for another year was profoundly depressing.

"And yet hope is one of the three chief Christian virtues," William reminded himself. He must not give up hope. Dr. Thomas hadn't. But it seemed now the exuberant doctor was so overly optimistic he got himself in constant difficulties. And how William hated to face Andrew Fuller and other such stalwarts who had helped him. How he had wanted to justify their faith in him.

"By Jove, Brother Carey," said Dr. Thomas excitedly after milling with seamen at a coffeehouse in London, "I think I'm on to another ship."

The next day they confirmed the fact that a Danish ship would anchor at Dover and take on passengers before it continued on to Calcutta! Without licenses. It seemed miraculous. But there was a catch. The two men didn't have enough money for the passage.

"We have enough money for you and Felix," said Thomas. "I'll book the two of you."

"No, sir," replied William. "We all three must go to India."

"Then we'll just have to go back to the society and ask them for more money," said Thomas cheerily.

"Yes, of course," said William numbly. "Come on, Felix," he said, forcing a smile, "we are going to Hackleton to visit Mother. And won't you be happy to see Willy and Peter and your new baby brother Jabez too?"

Thomas brightened. "I say, Brother Carey, now that your wife has had the baby perhaps she and the children will join us."

"Dr. Thomas! That would be four more fares to pay for."

"But we're asking the mission society for more money anyway," explained Thomas with his exuberant logic. "I knew this misfortune of ours was just an opportunity in disguise."

They took an overnight coach to Northampton and walked on to Hackleton. Dolly was overjoyed to see them. Foreign lands like India had never been her dream. She seemed lighter than air. She showed them pink-faced, tightfisted baby Jabez. But she was brought crashing to earth when she realized the two men were once again trying to persuade her to go to India. She refused angrily.

"Mrs. Carey," pleaded Dr. Thomas, "you will regret this as long as you live. For I fear your family will be forever separated."

She hesitated. "No, sir, I can't go."

"We must go on to Andrew Fuller in Kettering now, Dr. Thomas," said William in dejection. "We have very little time."

The two men and Felix left for Kettering. William was drained. Thomas seemed to be getting livelier and livelier. It was as if the worse things became the more he relished it. And on the way to Kettering Thomas stopped.

"You know, Brother Carey," he said, "I believe your wife was ready to say yes."

"Oh, what an optimist you are!" cried William, with no admiration. It was all he could do to keep from calling Thomas a fool. "I tried for months to get her to go to India."

"I'm going back," said Thomas.

William and Felix trudged back to Hackleton with Dr. Thomas. Dolly's jaw dropped as they entered the cottage. Her sister Kitty shook her head in disbelief. Thomas smiled and sat down. His face became very sober.

"I pray that God will make known His will to us this morning," he prayed. "Let us know, Lord, what to do."

"I've already told you," said Dolly sulkily.

"And I repeat, dear lady, that you will regret this decision to divide your family as long as you live."

Fear paled Dolly's face. "I don't want that. . ."

"Trust God," said Dr. Thomas softly.

"If Kitty would go, then maybe. . ."

"Kitty?" said the doctor, looking at Kitty for her answer.

"I must be alone for a few minutes," Kitty answered fearfully and stumbled into a bedroom.

William knew Kitty was praying. He was amazed at Dr. Thomas. The man had moved a mountain. He didn't doubt for a second now that somehow everything was going to work out. A few minutes later Kitty returned and they began packing. William and Thomas went on to Kettering.

"I feared this," said Andrew Fuller, as downcast as William had ever seen him. "You've failed."

"Not at all," said Thomas breezily. "My wife, daughter, and cousins are under way at this very moment. With our goods on board to finance our operations. We only came back for William's family."

"Mrs. Carey?" cried Andrew Fuller aghast.

"Of course now we have many more fares to pay for," said Thomas matter-of-factly. "Mrs. Carey, the three boys, and Mrs. Carey's sister Kitty."

Andrew Fuller blinked. "Five!"

"Yes sir, five." Thomas feigned surprise. "Well, didn't the society intend to send Brother Carey's family to India all along?"

"Of course," said Fuller, shaking his head. "It's just so unexpected. But in fact this development will save Brother Carey a trip back to England, won't it? And the society can't be accused of tearing a brother's family apart. I now see God's hand in this." Fuller assumed his bulldog look. "I don't see why the brothers can't raise additional funds."

William had hardly spoken since he left London. Dr. Thomas, seemingly defeated, seemingly disgraced, had stormed the walls of adversity like an Old Testament warrior and saved the day. And on June 13, 1793, the six were aboard the *Kron Princessa Maria* as the Danish ship lifted anchor and sailed into the Atlantic on a fair wind!

"Adieu, my dear brothers and sisters, adieu!" cried the exuberant Dr. John Thomas, gazing on the green of England. "Pray the God of Jacob be ours and yours, for time and eternity. Most affectionately farewell!"

William watched England disappear on the horizon. Would he ever see his homeland again? Some of his sorrow was lessened by his pleasure with the ship. Without saying so, he had been apprehensive about the *Kron Princessa Maria,* a Danish ship. But not now. It was a magnificent ship, as all "Indiamen"—as they were called by seamen—had to be, he learned. They were all well-staffed with a crew of about ninety, well-armed with about thirty cannons. They were swift yet carried enormous cargoes: precious English manufactured goods to India, then precious muslin, silks, spices, tea, and china back to England. Vast square sails billowed from three mainmasts.

"Let me introduce you to the captain of the *Kron Princessa Maria,*" chirped Thomas.

William turned to see a uniformed man with a billed

captain's hat. "I'm at your service, captain," said William and introduced Dolly and Kitty.

"I'm very pleased to have you aboard," said the captain.

"You're English!" exclaimed Kitty.

"I'm Danish," he corrected, then smiled. "But originally I was English, just as you thought. My half sister is Lady Langham of Cottesbrooke in your very own Midlands."

William was astonished to find that he and his family were lodged in the largest cabin on the ship. It was at the rear of the ship below the captain's poop deck. Thomas had a small first-class cabin nearby. The captain invited all of them to dine at his table. He asked about their welfare every day. What had Dr. Thomas told the captain to get such royal treatment? Would William ever get used to the volatile doctor's surprises, both bad and good?

"I was a wild boy," Thomas confided to William one afternoon while they were studying Bengali together. "School was an anathema to me. I hunted, fished, hiked, did anything but read books. You can imagine my family's shock when I made it through my medical training. They thought at long last I had matured. But no. I made a thorough mess of every medical practice I tried in London, so much in debt that I shipped out to India as a ship's doctor aboard the *Earl of Oxford*. My debts haunt me to this very day."

"In Calcutta too?" asked a worried William.

"It wasn't always my fault," answered Thomas evasively. "I was robbed and cheated a few times."

"Well, thanks for confiding in me, Brother Thomas," said William.

"I'm not through. You might as well know my other faults. My righteousness and enthusiasm have cost me many friends.

Both by writing and by tongue, I've launched many uncharitable, unmollified, hard-carved words at faltering brothers. In England and India."

"I too have failings," said William. "Just lately, though I've spent much time in prayer, I've felt dead to the Spirit. And I despair. How can I expect to be of any use to the heathen with such a barrenness in my own soul?"

"We perfectly complement each other then," concluded Thomas. "For I soar too high and you soar too low."

"You are always the optimist, brother. Praise God for that. It seems like only yesterday I wondered if I would ever see Dolly and the children again. Then I thought our mission was an utter failure. And now this royal treatment!"

The two men began to study Bengali. It comforted William to learn its symbols were written horizontally from left to right, like all the European languages. And words were separated by a space. Also, Thomas assured him Bengali was phonetic in that each symbol of its alphabet corresponded to a defined sound. However, the symbols were startling in their foreignness.

"Well, I've mastered Greek's unique alphabet," William reminded himself. "How many vowel symbols are there?" he asked Thomas.

"Eleven," answered Thomas. Anticipating William's next question he added, "There are thirty-three consonants. Oh, and there are thirteen vowel/consonant combinations to learn."

"Fifty-seven in all?"

"More or less," replied Thomas, "but let's not go too far too fast."

"If it is God's wish, I will learn this language, Doctor. And will its alphabet also serve to learn Hindi?"

"I'm afraid not. Hindi has its own alphabet." Then Thomas added brightly, "But the alphabet you learn for Hindi also serves Sanskrit!"

In the mornings and evenings and Sundays William led a worship service in their large cabin for their own eight and a fairly constant dozen others. They even formed a choir to sing hymns. It was a joy too for a linguist like William to hear Danish, Norwegian, German, and French spoken every day by passengers and crew. But too often from the mouths of the crew he also heard coarse talk about wine and loose women. He worried about his boys hearing such talk.

"Perhaps its best the boys do hear such gross carnality on the ship," said Thomas, the optimist, "for here you can correct their notions about such things."

In the Bay of Biscay, notched into France and Spain, the seas were so rough the *Kron Princessa Maria* could not pick up its mail. So the ship scudded on south along the African coast, although for a while it drifted far west, almost to Brazil. Then they encountered the westerlies that shot them east toward Capetown on the southern tip of Africa. They never put into port once. So William began to think the captain was worried about starting off for India too late in the season. He kept that worry to himself, as well as concern about his own bouts with diarrhea. All his fellow missionaries bore the trip well, no one better than tiny Jabez. A black woman and her infant were not so fortunate. They died before the *Kron Princessa Maria* could reach Capetown. The entire ship offered up their prayers as their bodies were claimed by the deep.

"Surely we will stop at Capetown," speculated William.

"Perhaps we should," added Thomas. "It looks stormy beyond."

But they did not stop. The ship rounded the cape and rode the favorable winds and currents northeast. Then a storm hit them so suddenly in the middle of the night it seemed a nightmare. *Praise God,* thought William, *they had not seen it coming sooner.* Anxiety tore so savagely at a fearful person, and no one seemed more fearful than Dolly. "At least she was spared hours of that," he thought. During the storm she hugged Kitty and wailed in terror. William felt fear too and prayed for forgiveness.

Thomas finally came to their cabin. "I've ridden out many a storm at sea, ladies," he said, smiling.

But the women were inconsolable. Next morning the seas seemed mountainous. Even Thomas, now pale-faced, had nothing cheery to say. Hours later as the rolling and pitching subsided, William and Thomas ventured on deck. All the sails had been taken down. Spars and rigging were in tatters.

"We've taken a bit of a battering," the captain told them.

The ship drifted without sail as the crew repaired the damage. "We could have been in Capetown all this time," complained Kitty. "Or Hackleton," said Dolly disagreeably. Thomas demonstrated his lack of tact, observing to William that Dolly was as difficult and headstrong as "Lot's wife." Eleven days later they lifted sail and scudded before the winds. William kept a log, impressed by the speed they made. But at one point Felix commented that he had not seen another ship in weeks.

William did not want to think what that might mean on such a well-traveled route.

eight

T he air warmed and bore earthy smells of land. Yet, as they neared India, William noticed the ship seemed to be moving ever slower. This continued day after day. The winds had not yet turned against them, as some feared, but the winds weakened and the ship fought strong currents of great Indian rivers rushing into the Bay of Bengal.

One morning Felix burst into the cabin. "Someone in the crow's nest says he can see Calcutta. The crew is working like mad on the rigging, tacking us northeast, then northwest. The sails have to be changed constantly. The sailors say they can never rest now."

"Has the wind changed now too?" asked Dolly, her voice choked with fear. Her eyes seemed glazed. "We've been at sea more than four months."

William said to Felix, "Let's go on deck for a spell."

On deck Felix continued grimly, "The crew says we'll be pushed all the way back to Vizagapatam."

"Well, we must all pray then," said William, "and not alarm the ladies."

A few days later a ship's carpenter died of pleurisy. A third body was claimed by the voyage. William prayed it was their last sacrifice to the sea. And at long last the ship entered the Hooghly River, gaping wide between lush green banks. The brown river whispered of heavy rain and fertile soil. One dawn in early November when they rushed to the rail of the ship they saw a sprawling city of palms and low buildings with red-tiled roofs. India seemed tinged reds and browns. Far upriver were pale columned buildings. Slender boats bobbed all around the ship. In the boats were dark-skinned, black-haired men wearing only turbans on their heads and cloths around their waists. They clutched long oars. All were lean and tightly muscled. They were gesticulating and yelling at the ship.

"So that's what they look like," said Dolly.

"The East Indians are handsome people," said William. "I was doubtful because of the derogatory way some of the crew talked about them."

"Macher jhol! Macher jhol!" yelled the boatmen.

"Say! I believe I understood that," said William in amazement. "Yes, see there, Dolly, they are selling fish!"

For hours the ship crawled up the river into the heart of Calcutta. The air was warm and sticky. More and more often they saw ramps down to the water. With increasing frequency the ramps were actually steps of stone. On shore behind the steps loomed more and more large imposing buildings of European design.

Finally Thomas came to William. "I've just come from the captain. We're going to be put off the ship here. He's hired some of these small boats to take us ashore."

Thomas did not have to explain why they were being put off the *Kron Princessa Maria* before it reached the main docks. They did not have licenses to enter India. Why invite trouble? William found the captain, shouting orders at the crew now with few pauses, and thanked him for his hospitality. Soon the eight, with their baggage, were transported ashore. Calcutta was stunning. Modern buildings of stone and brick stood everywhere, of obvious European design. Yet the open spaces were clogged with dark-skinned Indians. Cool, dark colors were not to be seen in their clothing. Instead, fabrics blazed bright oranges and greens and blues. Loops of brass and copper glittered everywhere because the Indians wore much in the way of bracelets and rings in the nose and ears.

"Sahibs!" screamed someone, looking at the party leaving the small boats.

Then some screamed, "Memsahibs!" and in great excitement pointed at Dolly and her sister.

The missionaries had gone ashore at a very large market. Indians milled about, buying cloth and jewelry and food. Familiar ginger, mint, and garlic wafted in the air but unknown exotic spices teased William's nose too. His legs wobbled as if he were still on the rolling, bobbing ship. To his amazement Dr. Thomas advanced into the midst of the market and began to preach. People gathered to listen. That was a very encouraging sign to William. The Indians were smiling too, white teeth dazzling in dark faces. Thomas preached for a very long time. After his long sermon some Indians approached the travelers to offer them curry and rice on large plantain leaves.

"Come to our village," they said earnestly.

William learned Thomas had already made various arrangements. He had sent a messenger to the house where his wife and the three others were staying. They were to meet the new arrivals north of Calcutta in a Portuguese settlement called Bandel. Soon Thomas and the Careys were being paddled up the Hooghly in boats Thomas had hired. In Bandel lived an old Swedish missionary named Kiernander. Thomas told William all about the old man. Kiernander had not pre-empted their mission at all because he tended only to Eurasians in English. A few days after they arrived in Bandel Thomas was delighted to be reunited with his wife and daughter again. But his wife had bad news.

"Your convert, Ram Ram Basu, has backslid, dear," she informed him.

"No."

"His own people shunned him because he betrayed them," she explained.

"But I explained to him that would happen. . ."

"And the English community shunned him too."

"I see," said Thomas sadly. "I had hoped for better."

"Well, he's welcome here," said William. "I want to hire him as my pundit. He will perfect my Bengali."

The energetic Thomas soon had William and Ram Ram Basu with him as he began itinerant preaching. They traveled by boat and by foot to the small villages in the riverine countryside. It seemed watery rice paddies glimmered everywhere. Most of the villagers were Hindus, but a few were Muslims. William quickly learned to distinguish which of the two sects an Indian claimed. Except for the handful of wealthy Indians who wore a variety of silks and brocaded clothes the peasants of the two religious cultures dressed in simple cotton cloth but quite differently. The Hindus wore clothing that "draped," the Muslims "tailored."

A Hindu man wore a dhoti, a rectangle of cotton cloth wrapped around the waist and securely tucked. He was uncovered above the waist. The Hindu woman also wore one rectangle of cloth, a sari, but it was much longer. Once the sari was wrapped securely around the waist twice it was brought up across the chest and over the left shoulder. The remainder hung down the back or was brought up to cover the head. The cotton cloth for the sari had one decorated border. In contrast the Muslims wore tailored clothing, the tops called "choli" and the bottoms loose but gathered tight at the ankles. The men usually wore turbans. The women added clothes to cover the head as well as give the clothing a more draped appearance. The face was covered by a veil.

William was impressed by the politeness of the Indians, their attentiveness to visitors and their ingrained religiosity. Flowers and Hindu shrines were seen all over the backcountry. But evidence of other practices hinted at by the professor in Leicester soon surfaced.

"Do you see the great scars on that man's back?" asked Thomas one day.

"They are monstrous," gasped William. "Crocodile?"

"They are from flesh hooks." And William was aghast as Thomas went on to explain how at religious festivals like the Doljatra, men of the lower castes were raised off the ground by ropes tied to hooks that pierced the man's back. High in the air the man was rotated on a horizontal arm as he scattered herbs offered to Shiva, one of the chief Hindu gods.

"How barbaric," muttered William in disbelief.

"And I'm hard pressed to know if it is a religious experience for the poor man or just an opportunity for him to make money," said Thomas, "because the heartbreaking sight will pull the last penny out of your pocket. Just to get the man to stop."

"That practice and many others have no basis in our sacred Hindu writings, the Shastras," said Ram Ram Basu defensively.

"Then perhaps we can eradicate these practices," said William."

"By Jove, we will!" exclaimed Thomas.

All through December the men visited villages and planned. But at Bandel, Felix, then Dolly, became very sick with what was called the "bloody flux." It was a form of diarrhea so severe it was accompanied by blood. It was the bane of foreigners in India. No one knew exactly what caused it. The supposed cure was almost as repulsive as the illness. Leeches were put on the stomach. Dolly tried hard to bear the illness without complaining. But Kitty complained for her.

"A jackal took Mrs. Thomas's dog," Kitty told William one evening in a tone of "just what do you intend to do about it?"

"A dog is not practical while living like this," he answered, secretly worrying that the predator might have been a leopard.

"That's true, I suppose," countered Kitty, "since there is not enough food for the children. Look at how ill poor Felix is."

William was now used to the bickering. Much of it he attributed to two sisters who felt as if they could say anything to each other. It would not get worse, he was sure, if he could just get them settled somewhere. Bandel was only temporary. He had heard about free land for settlers from a moneylender named Nelu Datta. And until the land could be procured the moneylender would allow them to live in a small house he had in Manicktullo, another rural area north of Calcutta.

"And where are the Thomases?" asked Kitty.

"He's setting up practice in Calcutta," admitted William. "He wants to make sure we don't run out of money."

The goods they brought to India to sell didn't bring in as much money as they thought they would. And because the

Careys had left Hackleton so abruptly they had no furniture or dishes. Indeed, they had forgotten much clothing. All those items had to be purchased in India. Plus everyday living and hiring boats and pundits were more costly than they had planned. And Mrs. Thomas and the others had spent a lot of money in Calcutta while waiting for the others to arrive. The truth was that the missionaries were already almost out of money. William was not going to alarm Dolly and Kitty with that news.

But halfway through January the two women exploded. "We hear Dr. Thomas has rented a fine big house in Calcutta!" cried Kitty.

"With servants!" added Dolly.

"Well, he must attract patients," explained William.

But no explanation satisfied the two women. "I'm sure the Thomases are eating bread and not rice," muttered Kitty. "Probably sitting on the patio sipping tea this very moment," grumbled Dolly. It was all William could do to resist bitterness himself. The women did not know how he visited Englishmen in Calcutta during the day, only to be treated with contempt. Even a prominent clergyman to whom he had an introduction written by John Newton had refused to see him. And on his return to Manicktullo the two women now openly berated him.

In his diary he wrote:

> *I am in a strange land, alone, no Christian friend, a large family—and nothing to supply their wants. . . . I am dejected, not for my sake but my family's. . . . In the evening [I] poured out my soul to God; but still my burden continued. The next*

day [I] had a pleasant time in prayer to God in the
morning but afterwards the abusive treatment I
receive from her who should be a help to me quite
overcame my spirits. I was vexed, grieved, and
shocked. I am sorry for her who never was hearty
in the undertaking, her health has been much
impaired, and her fears are great, though five
parts of six are groundless. . . . Oh that I may have
wisdom from above. . .[1]

The burden was so great he no longer concealed it from
friends. To John Sutcliffe in Olney he wrote:

[the two women are]. . .unhappy in one of the
finest countries in the world, and lonely in the
midst of a hundred thousand people. These are
burdens and afflictions to me but I bless God that I
faint not. . .[2]

The Bible sustained him as he awaited opportunity. Only
when his soul was satiated with God's Word could he forget
his distress. Finally the free land materialized. It was east of
Calcutta. Apparently William's pundit was involved in the
arrangements. Ram Ram Basu's uncle had been a landlord
there once. Ram Ram Basu tried to explain how the previous
governor of India, Lord Cornwallis, had thrown the land situation into chaos with a new tax system called "Permanent
Settlement," but William could not follow his logic. All he
knew was that the government now seized land for failure to
pay taxes or that moneylenders seized the land when the
landowners could not pay back the loan they floated to pay

the taxes. Land ownership had once been permanent in a family, almost sacred. Now it was in total confusion.

William rushed into Calcutta to say farewell to Thomas. "They say a government bungalow is already there that we can use until we build our own," he said excitedly.

"And where is this land?" asked Thomas.

"East, in an area called the 'Sundarbans.' "

"The Sundarbans!"

"Do you know it?"

"I hunted there once," answered Thomas, much more solemn than usual.

"Oh, what did you hunt? Perhaps we can live on wild game."

"Listen, Brother Carey, why don't you remain in Manicktullo a little longer. Give me a chance to see if I can find something for you at Malda where I was stationed my last time in India. I've been negligent. I should have done that sooner. I'm terribly sorry. . ."

"Send word to the Sundarbans through the relatives of Ram Ram Basu," replied William. "I must get started."

On the evening of February 3, 1794, Carey, now thirty-two years old, Dolly, who had just turned thirty-eight, and Kitty, thirty, stepped into a boat with the boys: Felix, eight, Willy, five, and Peter, four. Dolly carried nine-month-old Jabez. Ram Ram Basu also went.

"We go to Debhatta," said Ram Ram Basu to the boatmen in Bengali.

The boatmen guided the loaded craft through a bewildering web of rivers. Some gaped wide. Some were barely navigable. The first night they anchored in what seemed a lake, but so shallow the boatmen easily reached the bottom with a pole.

"Are we going to sleep in the boat?" asked William.

"It's best," replied Ram Ram Basu.

"How odd." But sleeping on a boat was certainly not alarming to a family that had just spent five months at sea.

The next day they saw the terrain. It was nothing like any land William had ever seen. There seemed no grass, only mud. Yet on higher ground away from the rivers grew trees. The most common tree was the sundari, for which the Sundarbans were named. But the tamarind tree was there too, noted for very hard wood suitable for furniture and for fruity seed pods that could be eaten. Coconuts and bamboo grew there too, Ram Ram Basu assured them.

"After I plant my garden," William told Dolly, "we will have lentils, mustard, onions, and peas. Say, I thought I saw a deer in the distance."

"It's peculiar how far one can see back through the trees," commented Dolly. "It seems there is nothing from ground level up to the first branches of the trees."

They spent their days watching the mud banks roll by. A small fish of some kind actually slithered around on the mud bank, as if walking on its fins, then popped back into the water. Crabs skittered about the mud surface too. That night the travelers once again anchored in the river, not at the edge but in the middle.

"Do we sleep in the boat again?" said William in surprise.

"It's best," replied Ram Ram Basu.

The next day they saw a sight they were unprepared for. A great green reptile as long as the boat lay on the mud bank. It was a crocodile, sides bulging, watching them through primeval yellow eyes. Huge spikes of teeth poked out of its closed jaws. William assured Dolly and Kitty the beast could not get to them. But he was not so sure.

"Now I know why we don't camp on shore at night," groaned Kitty.

"It's not a good idea," agreed Ram Ram Basu.

That night William thought he heard a distant roar. Leopard? Tiger? He didn't know. Of course he had heard Indians speak of tigers, but they were rare around settlements. The big solitary killers learned to stay clear of settlements. But where were the settlements?

Kitty had noticed too. Next morning she asked Ram Ram Basu, "Where are all the people?"

"None live here," he replied. "In this area men come only to cut wood or collect wild honey. They live in villages somewhere else."

Finally the missionaries arrived at their destination. Up on a rise away from the river, here called the Jubuna, was a village. Debhatta, it was named. The few villagers they saw were clearly all Muslims from their dress. And there was indeed a government bungalow—brick too, with a verandah. Trees had been cleared around the neat bungalow, but, although huts could be seen here and there, the surroundings looked suspiciously like the grim forest they had seen for the last few days. Dolly could not hide her disappointment. She looked as if she would protest, but glanced at the boys and remained silent.

"Good Heavens," was all Kitty could say.

"It just needs a green thumb to brighten the place," said William.

As grim as the muddy forest appeared, the travelers were only too pleased to get off the boat, climb the mud bank and walk around. A man rushed out of the brick bungalow, smiling. He was a government official named Charles Short. He was already living in the bungalow!

"But you are welcome to join me," he assured them. "I wouldn't think of your staying anywhere else."

So they moved their belongings into the bungalow. While the women were preparing food for the children inside the bungalow Charles Short took William for a walk. They didn't go far. Short was carrying a very large muzzle loader.

"Game so close to the house?" asked William. "Say, I was wondering about the hunting here. We've almost forgotten what meat tastes like."

"Actually, it's for protection, Reverend."

"Protection?"

"Tigers."

"I thought tigers avoided people."

"Not here in the Sundarbans they don't. People avoid tigers. Tigers killed twenty people last year in this district alone."

"I see." Fear crawled on William.

"Needless to say, you will have to keep your boys close to the house."

"What should I tell the women?"

"Just tell them there are snakes about. That's true enough too. There's a mangrove cobra here who is a nasty fellow. But you can usually get away from a snake. You can't escape a tiger." Short paused a moment. "They say there's something wrong with these tigers they way they hunt people. Something in the water perhaps. I don't know."

"Will the tiger come up to the house at night?"

"None has yet. Not in Debhatta."

"These people appear to be mostly Muslims," mused William. "I've asked my fellow Englishmen many questions about Hindus but not Muslims."

"Well, they don't rely so heavily on vegetables like the Hindus. Much of their custom is Jewish in origin. It seems the only things they can't eat are blood and pork. Seven days after birth a baby is named in a ceremony called 'aqiqah.' Between the ages of seven and twelve, the boys are circumcised. Marriage is important and a man may have as many as four wives if he treats them as equals. For the dead, a service is given before burial. In the grave, the face of the corpse faces their holy city of Mecca."

"And what does this word Sunnite mean?"

"Oh, I see you know more about Muslims than I assumed. Well, as I understand it Muslims are largely divided into Sunnites and Shiites. The Shiites are mystics and can be quite violent. The Sunnites are more pious, more accommodating. Thank God that India has Sunnites."

That evening William told the women and boys about the snakes. Both women locked resentful eyes on his face. They held their tongues because Charles Short was eating with them. William told them they should not venture far from the house and if they did they should peer far back into the forest. There might be a wild hog or something he could shoot for food, he added lamely.

"And don't let the boys play near the edge of the river," added Charles Short quickly, "because of the crocodiles."

"I say, Reverend," Charles Short asked William later, "do you know where your land is located?"

"I thought this was it."

"Well, no. Actually this land and bungalow belong to the salt works run by the East India Company. We have a warehouse here. I manage it."

"I see."

The next day Ram Ram Basu took William to his land. It was not in Debhatta, but one mile north on the Jubuna River. Supposedly there was a village there too called Kalutala. But the locale seemed barren of anything but the grim forest.

"Once you get settled here, sahib," said Ram Ram Basu, "other people will come here too. I will spread the word. You will see."

Ram Ram Basu continued as William's pundit. But William had much physical labor to do. He and Felix walked to their land each day and cleared it. Although Dolly's "bloody flux" lingered, Felix was healthy again. They were careful to preserve the larger tamarinds and sundaris as well as banyans, mangoes, and coconuts. The two laid out a garden, then William paced off the dimensions for a house. The house, built on stilts high off the ground, would be framed and floored with bamboo, then walled and roofed with mats.

"Look, Father," said Felix one day as they worked.

"Why, it's the others."

William was angry. He had told them not to come. But he had been evasive as to why they should not. How many days could he come to their land without expecting them to follow? So he welcomed them and let them stroll about. Dolly refused. Tight-lipped, she stood near the bamboo frame, holding Jabez. Meanwhile Willy saw a golden-backed woodpecker. Peter found a small harmless snake. Kitty found something too.

"Come quick!" she cried. "I've found some very large tracks."

William looked at them. The hair rose on the back of his neck.

nine

*E*ach of the tracks Kitty had found registered a heel mark and four toes. The tracks were not symmetrical like a dog's. They were almost as large as a plate in the soft mud.

"So big! I'll bet its a rhinoceros!" exclaimed Willy.

"It's not a cat, is it?" asked Dolly, who had joined them.

"How could it be?" quickly answered Kitty. "There are no claw marks."

But William knew cats retract their claws. He had studied many tracks in the English countryside as a boy, often with his uncle Peter. These huge tracks were most certainly from a cat. And only one cat was large enough to leave tracks so large one could not so foolishly think they were left by a rhinoceros.

"Tiger," said Ram Ram Basu, who just appeared.

"Tiger!" screamed Dolly.

"Yes," commented William weakly.

That evening on the verandah Dolly scowled at William. "Tell me this is a nightmare. Tell me I'm going to wake up back in England." She clutched the infant Jabez as she aimed her despair at the Sundarbans. "This terrible black forest surrounds us like a death shroud."

William brushed off her comment. "The boys are already asleep, Dolly," he said. "Where is Charles Short this evening?"

"He left about noon to visit some sites where the natives process salt."

"Where is Kitty?"

"Helping the Indian boys gather wood, I am sure. We agreed we must not let the fires go out. Ever." She shuddered.

In the eery orange glow they now saw shadowy forms of Bengalis piling wood between the fires. Dolly's eyes softened as she saw her sister Kitty appear, throw down an armload of wood and climb onto the verandah. She looked as frightened as Dolly.

"One of the Indian boys says we must not pile any more wood," said Kitty. "Why?" She looked at William angrily as if she expected he would lie to her no matter what.

William was tired of trying to smooth things over. It was impossible in such a place. So he said simply, "Piles of wood on this barren ground attract cobras."

"Poisonous snakes," muttered Kitty. "What else?"

"I am going to pray every moment of every day for God to deliver me from this place," muttered Dolly as she rose to put Jabez to bed.

One evening several days later William came back to the bungalow from their property well satisfied. The bamboo house was almost done. But how could he tell Dolly? And how could he tell the younger boys? Dolly had told the boys the story of the three little pigs with a particular vengeance the night before. How would they react to living in a straw house instead of a brick house?

"You have some mail, Reverend," announced Charles Short.

"Thank you. Say, it's from Dr. Thomas."

"Oh, how are things at his mansion?" asked Kitty not so innocently.

William read the letter silently. The two sisters were touchy about the doctor. William was only amused. Dr. Thomas seemed his best friend and his worst enemy—all rolled into one person. In the letter Thomas said he had been talking to old friends, the Udnys, at Malda. George Udny was now an important East India Company official there, one entrusted with encouraging business enterprises. Would Dr. Thomas be interested in running an indigo processing plant near Malda? he had asked. The blue dye was in great demand. The English couldn't build the plants fast enough. The salary was fixed and quite substantial. The plant manager would have a nice house, even servants. So Thomas had agreed to run the indigo plant at Mahipaldighi.

"That Dr. Thomas is a lucky rascal to be sure," said William.

"We're so happy for him," commented Kitty.

William read on. He blinked. What was this Thomas had written? Would William be interested in running a similar plant near Mudnabati? The generous salary would be the same! And William too would have a nice house and servants. Udny believed he could even pull strings to get the two men licenses, so at last they would be free from the threat of being arrested. If William was interested, he must write Thomas at once. Then Thomas would send him the money to make the three-hundred-mile trip north.

William put the letter down. "You must have done some powerful praying, Dolly."

"What do you mean?" She smiled for the first time in weeks.

He read the letter aloud. Dolly was almost hysterical with happiness. She only frowned as she realized the departure from Debhatta would be several weeks away. Dr. Thomas had to wait for William's reply. Then the Careys had to wait for money to arrive from Thomas. In his diary William rationalized:

> *Though I have the great pleasure of hoping the mission (here in Debhatta) may be abundantly forwarded by having a number of the natives under my direct inspection, and at the same time my family be well provided for, though I have no doubt respecting provision even here, yet a too great part of my time must have necessarily been employed in managing my little farm with my own hands; I shall likewise be joined with my colleague (Dr. Thomas) again (in Mudnabati), and we shall unitedly engage in our work.*[1]

Charles Short explained that the new governor of the East India Company, Sir John Shore, might have had something to do with these new opportunities found by Dr. Thomas.

"Of course," said William, remembering. "I believe he was a member of the Clapham Sect in London with Charles Grant and William Wilberforce. These powerful gentlemen all were supposedly very receptive to converting the heathens."

"Pray then India stays at peace," said Charles Short. "Because if there is any threat to English interests from the natives or from France the Crown will send a governor like Cornwallis again."

"A military man," concluded William.

Dolly's joy over the move was short-lived. She learned Charles Short had proposed to Kitty. And Kitty had accepted.

They would be living both in Debhatta and in Calcutta. Dolly was dazed.

"How did I not know?" she asked William and became more outspoken than ever. "How I detest India!"

William abandoned his bamboo house. He spent all his time learning Bengali, which he described as a "very copious language, abounding with beauties." For a long time his mouth had been shut, he told himself, and his days beclouded with heaviness. But the hope of mastering Bengali put fresh life into his soul. He felt once again like a voyager, who had almost perished in a violent storm, but who, with dripping, battered clothes, sees blue sky breaking through the gray clouds.

But William often found himself back in the storm. Ram Ram Basu had been enthusiastically recruiting Indians all around the Sundarbans to come to Kalutala. According to him, several hundred had already agreed. Thousands would follow. Was William abandoning thousands of Indians crying out for protection? Thousands of heathens who could be converted to Christ? Each day William waited for Thomas's reply he grew more depressed. In the back of his mind was the anxiety over the yet unknown monsoons. Things became difficult when the rains started, Ram Ram Basu said. Journeying upriver in the rainy season just might be impossible. Usually the drenching rains began in late May and early June, but they could begin sooner. And so the chance of being marooned by the monsoons gnawed at William. He was loaded down with guilt too. Had he in Debhatta failed again?

> *My soul is a jungle, when it ought to be a garden. I can scarcely tell whether I have the grace of God or no[t]. How shall I help India, with so*

little Godliness myself?[2]

But prayer and the Bible bolstered him, and soon he would write:

> *When I first left England my hope of the conversion was very strong, but amongst so many obstacles it would entirely die away, unless upheld by God—nothing to exercise it, but many things to obstruct it for now a year and 19 days, which is the space since I left my dear charge in Leicester; since then I have had hurrying up and down; a five month imprisonment with carnal men on board the ship, five more learning the language; my Moonshee [Ram Ram Basu] not understanding English sufficiently to interpret my preaching—my family my accusers, and hinderers, my colleague separated from me, long delays, and few opportunities for social worship. . .no woods to retire to. . .for fear of Tygers. . .no earthly thing to depend upon, or earthly comfort; except food and raiment; well, I have God, and His Word is sure. . .*[3]

And so his mind was calmed by his faith in God, yet seethed with doubt in himself and his family. Even if the superstitions of the heathen were a thousand times stronger than they are, he told himself, and the example of the Europeans a thousand times worse than they are, even if he were deserted by all and persecuted by all, yet his faith, fixed on that sure Word, would rise above all obstructions and overcome every trial. "God's cause will triumph," he kept telling himself.

By the beginning of May he was so disturbed by Dolly's constant unhappiness, often goaded into great outbursts of complaining by unthinking Kitty, he wrote:

> *I have none of those helps and encouragements from my family that many have—they are rather enemies to the work that I have undertaken but though I find it extremely difficult to know how to act with propriety, and sometimes perhaps act indiscreetly, yet I find that support in God which I can find no where else, and perhaps these trials are designed to put me upon trusting and seeking happiness from the Lord alone.*[4]

Every time he saw Dolly now it seemed she complained, sometimes in screams of anguish. She, who despised India, had learned that during the summer monsoons India was even worse than it was now. Flooding, heat. Disease and death magnified a thousand times! William could see the resentment and fear eating at Dolly. She had steadfastly refused to come to India, insisting she would hate it. Then in one weak moment she was whisked away before she could change her mind again. How she hated her fate. And her "captors." And now Kitty, her one consolation it seemed, was being taken away from her. William felt very guilty now about Thomas's browbeating Dolly into coming. How much more peaceful it would have been without her. And he felt guilty about feeling that way too.

"Dolly wasn't always this way," he explained lamely to

Charles Short after one of her bitter tirades.

"Of course, Reverend," answered Short, who could think of nothing to add.

And so, as William honed his skill at Bengali, his thoughts vacillated from triumph to failure. "Expect great things from God; attempt great things for God," he reminded himself. And what could be more ambitious, festering in a muddy forest with a distraught wife, than to begin translating the Bible into Bengali? But that was exactly what he began to do with Ram Ram Basu's help. He even traipsed to a temple with Ram Ram Basu and debated two Brahmins in front of about two hundred natives. His mission never seemed more right as he heard the Brahmins explain the wooden image of a man riding on the back of a tiger was Dukkinroy, the god of the woods, and the wooden image of a headless woman riding a headless horse was Sheetulla, the goddess of smallpox.

"This is idolatry," he told them in stumbling words with the help of Ram Ram Basu. "It is wicked."

And he went on to try to explain how the only way to salvation was through Christ. But as he left them he felt depressed. What had he accomplished? He was going to be leaving these people in a few short weeks, maybe days. Was he merely undermining the faith they had? After all, didn't they have "laws" similar to the Ten Commandments? Perhaps their "laws" had not been presented in such a compact and obligatory way but still they seemed to be there, submersed in that vast milieu of Hinduism:

> *Utter not a word by which anyone could be*
> *wounded.*
> *He who is cruel and calumnious has the character*

of a cat.

He who is asked for alms should always give.

*For him who fails to honor his father and mother,
every work of piety is in vain.*

*Children, old men, the poor, and the sick should
be considered the lords of the atmosphere.*

*A sacrifice is obliterated by a lie and the merit of
alms by an act of fraud.*

*One should never strike a woman, not even with
a flower.*

Oh, yes. Somewhere in the vast conglomeration of Hinduism was a holiness, a right way to live. So William felt guilty about attacking their beliefs, not because the true way was not through Christ, but because he attacked their beliefs without staying to lead them to Christ. And the only relief of his guilt about his bumbling efforts and his difficulty with Dolly came from his faith.

He simply had to trust God. "When I reflect, Lord," he prayed, "how You stirred me up into this work and how You prepared my way, then I can trust Your promises and be at peace that this work is part of Your plan."

At last the money came from Thomas. It was nearly the last week in May, the traditional start of the monsoons. William hurriedly loaded a large, canopied boat he had hired in advance. Dolly had been assured by Charles Short that the wedding would take place in Debhatta in a few months. Meanwhile Kitty would live with relatives of Ram Ram Basu. So on the dawn of May 23, 1794, without Kitty, the Careys headed north through a maze of rivers: the Jubuna, then the Isamuti, then the Jellinghi. Dolly seemed pacified by the obvious activity on and along the river. Boats with cargoes floated by. Men in boats hauled in fishing nets. And the banks teemed with colorful, busy Indians too. Pungent smells of spices reached the travelers. Wildlife chirped and squawked, endearing and harmless from a distance.

"Please, Lord, speed us on to do your work," prayed William every day as he watched the increasingly cloudy skies for rain that might slow them, even stop them.

He hid his anxiety from the family and translated the Bible into Bengali, trying not to be irritated by the boys' constant chatter that often erupted into scrapping. Three hundred miles in such a boat was no short trip. After many days they floated into the mighty Ganges, here not as muddy, and so wide it seemed a sea. The current was so strong they had be towed up river. At Nabobganj they slipped up the Mahanadi River. At last they spotted their first destination: Malda. It was June 15. The trip took twenty-three days.

The Careys were welcomed warmly by the George Udnys. Word was sent to Mahipaldighi so Thomas could welcome them too. On Sunday William preached in English to a tiny congregation. "My joy is indescribable," he told them, "in being at last set free to fully preach the Gospel." Yet he knew preaching in English was just an indulgence. The future required Bengali and as many other tongues as he could master.

"Please inquire about our letters from England," Dolly asked William stonily.

Later, with faint hope, he asked Thomas if he had heard anything from the brothers in England yet. "My dear fellow," replied Thomas. "The brothers are only now getting *our* first letters from India. We won't get a reply for many months." And Thomas returned to Mahipaldighi.

While Dolly and the boys relaxed in the plantation life of the Udny home, William went with George Udny to learn the indigo business. They visited several local processors. June was the month the natives cut and bundled the indigo stalks and brought them to the processing plants. They were dumped into upper vats full of water to ferment. Eventually the water would turn dark green, William was told. At the proper time the water was drained into lower vats where natives thrashed it constantly with paddles to aerate it. The water turned from dark green into dark blue. Again, at the proper time, the liquid was allowed to rest, William was told, so crystals of the blue dye would settle to the bottom of the vats. Then the water was drawn off and the crystalline sediment purified further by boiling, eventually yielding cubes for shipment. And why was this product in such demand? Because indigo alone dyed cloth a rich blue that lasted wash after wash.

"So you see, Reverend," said George Udny, "with experience, the entire process, though involved, is very straightforward—and very profitable."

In August the Careys went by boat up the Tangan River to Mudnabati. This boat too was large and canopied. So in spite of rain the scenery was pleasant. The area they saw was not forested but cleared. It was a watery world of rivers and fields of rice or indigo. White-clothed natives shot their small dugouts all over the rivers and the watery fields. Bamboo clusters were scattered about too. Trees seemed confined to small villages on hills. At Mudnabati they found their home.

"Brand new. Two-story. Brick too," gushed Dolly approvingly.

114

"Be careful, boys," cautioned William as the three boys stormed around their new surroundings.

"Be careful of what?" asked Dolly, with fear in her eyes.

"They tell me only snakes are a danger here." He smiled encouragement. "They say the crocodiles here are large but of a mild temper. They may steal a chicken or two."

"No tigers?" she asked. Her eyes were deathly cold. It seemed she would never forgive William for tigers.

"No tigers."

The inside of the house pleased Dolly. The rooms were spacious and the windows large. Beyond the house sprawled the processing plant along the river. The plant itself was still under construction. A large raised reservoir of water filled by waterwheels from the river was finished. Completed also were the five pairs of vats to which the reservoir fed water. So the five upper vats were at that very time receiving bundles of indigo plants brought in by boats and by oxcarts. By the time the lower vats were drained to reveal their rich blue sediment the rest of the works was expected to be finished. That included boilers, furnaces, and warehouses. William would supervise over two hundred workers when the processing plant was finished.

He wrote Andrew Fuller a letter describing their new venture and their new plans. How William planned now! Beside the house was a plot set aside for a garden. What he planned for those several acres could scarcely be called a garden. He ordered seeds and bulbs of dozens of kinds of vegetables, and cuttings of trees, both for fruit and wood. He ordered scythes, sickles, and plow parts. He requested Curtis's Botanical Magazine. Under the tutelage of Robert Brewin in Leicester William had became an "amateur" of English tradition, a botanist who knew as much as any professor. What a horticultural manifestation of God's creations he would capture in this fertile soil! As steward of God's gifts, he also intended to raise ducks, chickens, cattle, hogs, and sheep. These too he promptly set out to secure for his "farm." And soon he hoped to even have the luxury of a horse!

"Praise God," he said. "If, after God has so wonderfully made way for us, I should be negligent, the blackest brand of infamy must lie upon my soul."

He also continued to labor on his translation of the Bible into Bengali. By now William had discovered Ram Ram Basu was too polite, often approving a translation that fell short. So he had to rework passages. By November he hoped to have finished Genesis, Matthew, Mark, and James. This was very important. And its by-product was to be a mastery of Bengali sufficient to actually preach to the natives. How he longed for that great day.

The locals were not healthy. William soon realized that always a good portion of the workers were sick with some malady. The many servants in their house were sick too. They worked anyway. Poor people did not have the luxury of lying about on mats. William was already running headlong into their strange customs. At one stage of the indigo-making process his workers asked him to add an offering to the goddess Kali, the consort of one of their three great gods, Shiva. Kali was a ferocious goddess, depicted in idols as scowling with bloodstained teeth and wearing a necklace of human skulls. In one of her four arms she held the severed head of a man. A blood sacrifice to Kali protected the worshiper from catastrophe.

"No, I won't do it," William told his workers.

But he stopped short of preventing them from doing it. It was too soon to do that. As yet he had not given them the true Word of God. Never again would he undermine beliefs, even pagan beliefs, unless he could offer them Christ. So he silently watched his workers sacrifice a poor bleating goat to Kali. He had already discovered the kind of resistance to Christ he might encounter in this place. He had successfully hired servants for the house. But it was much harder than hiring workers for the plant because servants in the house came into direct contact with the English. For example, William had tried to hire a boy for the house who belonged to one of the lowest Hindu castes because he worked with animal hides in making sandals. But the boy accepted only after many refusals. He was afraid of what the other Hindus might do to him.

"So," deduced Dolly correctly, "our house servants are the lowest of the low in the eyes of their fellow Hindus or Muslims."

Muslims lived in the vicinity too. Only days after the Careys arrived they were surprised to see a hoard of people marching onto the property. Hundreds, perhaps a thousand. No, it was not a welcoming party. It was a Muslim holy day and it seemed the indigo plant was virtually on the spot where a Muslim saint was buried!

Indians were very curious too. So William was not surprised when many of the Muslims stopped to simply gawk awhile at the oddly dressed English invaders. Questions were not considered rude either.

"How much money do you make?" asked an old man.

"How did you lose your hair?" asked another.

"How do you bleach your skin?" asked a third.

William worked hard. And when the rainy season ended he planned to work even harder. That was when he would plant his garden. But by the middle of September he was felled by a fever unlike any the Careys had suffered yet.

ten

William's fever began like a common cold but soon pain racked his neck and back. His head throbbed pure agony. Dolly insisted he had a fever, yet William felt chills in the pained areas. Soon he could not keep food down. Ulcers formed around his mouth. Then he felt feverish but could not sweat to break the fever. Finally he did begin to sweat, a river it seemed. The bedding was soaked. Then he began to recover.

"What in the world was that?" he asked Dolly. "The infamous jungle fever?"

"If it is," she said with fear in her eyes, "I've heard it said that you will get it right back."

And so he did.

The symptoms of the cold started again with his neck aching. With his head pounding he thought he heard that Peter was sick too. He heard Dolly say in a very pessimistic voice that William had been shaking for twenty-six hours. "How much longer can this continue?" she whispered too loud. William's only consolation was that he was the one suffering this time, not Dolly. It seemed by the grace of God that George Udny happened to visit. And he had with him a vial of "bark," which was what they called quinine, a medicine extracted from the bark of the cinchona tree.

"I will show you how to mix it," Udny told Dolly and William. "It must be done carefully. It is a very strong poison."

And Udny showed them how to measure a tiny pinch of the "bark," then mix it with a much larger amount of a mild resin. "I've mixed six doses here." He poured a tiny amount into a spoon. "Here, William, take the first. I warn you. You may lose your hearing. But that is only temporary."

After a few doses of the "bark" William began to go deaf. Udny watched him closely. When he determined William was completely deaf the treatment was stopped. William soon regained his hearing. And the illness was gone. No chills, no fever, no aches.

"Was my illness then indeed the illness known in the tropics as 'jungle fever'?" he asked Udny.

"Yes," said Udny grimly. "You will have attacks of this jungle fever for the rest of your life. I have them myself. Don't run out of the 'bark.'"

"You are well enough now to know Peter is quite ill," Dolly told William, her face drained.

Five-year-old Peter? It seemed impossible. He was such a lively boy. Smart too. The child already spoke Bengali like a native to William's ears. But William's concerns for Peter were blunted when he suffered a severe relapse. It was not fever this time but severe vomiting and diarrhea. What was it this time? And how much of this latest affliction could William's body stand? Losing all nourishment he could not sustain himself. But soon it passed.

"Peter still has the 'flux' or whatever it is," said Dolly, fear in her eyes.

"We must pray for him," said William weakly.

Thomas came to doctor Peter but the child's body did not have the capacity to withstand a long onslaught of vomiting and diarrhea. In a daze William asked if Peter battled one of the many forms of dysentery that plagued India or had his dysentery been followed by an onslaught of the dread cholera that killed so suddenly? Was cholera what William had suffered himself in his sudden relapse? Cholera killed about half its victims in a few days or not at all. There were so many maladies in the tropics with the same symptoms of fever and vomiting and diarrhea it seemed impossible to tell one from another, admitted Thomas.

On October 11 Peter died.

"Peter, dead!" screamed Dolly.

How much more could she suffer? William soon learned. It was not enough that there was no faithful Kitty there to comfort her in her grief—not friends of any kind in Mudnabati— but William himself was completely distracted by problems with the burial. For it seemed no one would help.

"I can't get the carpenters at the plant to make us a coffin," William told Felix out of Dolly's hearing. "It seems that not only do both Hindus and Muslims refuse to touch the dead in any way but they will not assist in any way."

Finally he had to coerce four Muslim workers into digging a grave south of the plant, far away from any known Muslim graves. The next day William learned their headman had not only cast the four out of the village but had forbidden any villager to associate with them. Although it was completely against his nature, William went to the headman and threatened to have him arrested by English authorities unless he lifted his ban on the four men. Though successful, the confrontation took the whole day. And still William could find no pallbearers. It took another two days of arguments and threats before he found anyone to carry poor Peter's body to the grave. Finally two house servants agreed to do it: Matu, the one who cleaned their latrine, and a poor boy considered to have no caste at all. So the two servants carried Peter to the grave.

"Our darling boy, not even buried in a coffin," muttered Dolly, "and this filthy soil full of worms and such."

Never would William have imagined that he could get no help in burying Peter. They had so many servants. Too many, in his opinion. They were many because they insisted they could do no more than one task or they would anger their gods. The Careys employed two women millers, a baker, a cook, a butler, a nurse, a man to procure groceries, two handymen, housecleaners, several gardeners, one man to care for each kind of livestock, and even one man to collect the sap from date trees that served as yeast. If William could have kept Dolly from knowing the difficulty he was having with Peter's burial he would have. But he could not. He hadn't thought her eyes could get any colder toward him than they had when she mentioned tigers. But now her eyes were icy. She seemed a different woman; she was so remote.

"But the Hindus do throw their own dead in the river or burn them, don't they?" she said bitterly. "And the Muslims do bury their own dead, don't they? Don't we have the grave of one of their saints nearby? So, it's you they won't help, isn't it, William?"

George Udny rushed to console the Careys after he was notified. Immediately he insisted Dolly bring the boys and stay with his own family in Malda for several weeks. Meanwhile he sent William north with Thomas on the pretext of looking for sites suitable for indigo processing. But it was intended as relief from the strain of Peter's death and the indigo plantation. The men actually left Bengal to hunt in the region called Bhutan.

"Praise the Lord, look!" said William, pointing in the distance.

"The Himalayas!" said Thomas.

Mountaintops capped by snow loomed in the distance. William could scarcely fathom such immensities. One enormity straight north, said their guide, was perhaps the highest peak in the world. It was called Kanchenjunga. And yet the men now stood in the foothills, lush with forests, teeming with wild game. Thomas spoke excitedly of elephants, leopards, tigers, and bears. William was enthralled by the flora. Had it ever been described by an Englishman? He doubted it. Where would he start? Hundreds, thousands of kinds of plants flourished in this green paradise. William collected seed pods, roots, leaves. It was a floral treasure he could not exhaust. Meanwhile Thomas stalked the beasts of the forested hills. Once while they were boating up a river to find wild buffalo, a tiger burst from the brush to nearly jump into their vessel. The great beast didn't seem real to William; this cool, green world was aglut with so many wonders.

"Praise God," said William. "These moments alone make a trip halfway around the world worthwhile."

The people of Bhutan were very open and kind. At the town of a local ruler called a "suba" the two visitors were greeted in the name of the Grand Lama himself. A crowd of several thousand watched. Then in a large hall they were feted. William learned they had many books on astrology and religion in their language, which was a dialect of the mountain people of Tibet. The suba insisted the Bhutans worshipped "the greatest one seen only by the mind." Their priests were called "lamas." William returned to Malda excited and

123

refreshed.

Dolly was cold, but after all wasn't she still grieving? "We still have no letters from England," she informed William. "We've been in India for over one year. Explain to me again why we have no mail."

"I can't."

"The Udnys get mail. Does no one care about you?"

The Careys spent Christmas in Malda with the Udnys and returned to Mudnabati on New Year's Eve. Peter's death still stung William when he thought about it. But so had the deaths of his daughters. He had disciplined himself to remember the joyful things about them. God would surely want it that way. And it wasn't as if they weren't much better off. Naturally they were with the Lord. On the way back to Mudnabati William regaled the boys with tales of Bhutan. But later he was made to realize his enthusiasm about his trip to Bhutan was a mistake.

"It sounds as if you visited the Garden of Eden while the boys and I rotted in Malda," commented Dolly.

"I thought you enjoyed the company of the Udnys."

"Were the women in Bhutan to your taste?"

"The women? What a thought! The natives are Buddhists. They speak a peculiar dialect of the Tibetan language."

"You and your languages," she said bitterly.

He wrote in his journal:

> *This time have had bitters (of a family kind) mingled with my soul.*[1]

And then he did study his languages. Now he tackled Hindi as well as Bengali. He hired another pundit besides Ram

Ram Basu. Hindi had its own script just as Thomas had said. But there were some similarities. The sounds, and therefore the number of symbols, were nearly the same. Hindi was written in what was called the "Nagari" alphabet. At least this alphabet served more than one language, William learned. And they were very important languages in India. The sacred language of Sanskrit was in Nagari. So was the very important language of Marathi of central India.

"With these additional languages in tow the Gospel can be delivered far and wide in India," William said hopefully.

He resumed his demanding duties as overseer of the indigo plant too. The Indian winter was well under way. His bout with jungle fever had left him sensitive to cold. He had to wear a great coat and still felt chilled, even though the temperatures during the day reached more than seventy degrees. But that seemed the least of his worries. He found out a clerk had been swindling the workers out of five percent of their pay. He fired him immediately.

"I'll give these duties to someone I can trust," said William and gave them to Ram Ram Basu.

In unraveling the corruption William discovered the workers had been cheated so many ways in the past that they trusted no one. Landowners, moneylenders, and village headmen were notorious for their heavy-handed ways. Foremen at this very indigo plant had been cheating workers out of their wages. William fired them too. Many of his problems with the local people stemmed from a lack of trust, William concluded. He would make every effort to restore trust.

But lack of trust was a problem at home too. To his utter amazement Dolly continued to question his fidelity. In all other ways she acted rationally. That made her accusations even more astonishing. Every day when he returned from his plantation work she acted as if he had made some liaison with another woman. In early February he wrote for his own eyes only:

> *This is indeed the Valley of Death to me except that my soul is much more insensible than John Bunyan's Pilgrim. Oh, what would I give for a sympathetic friend such as I had in England, to whom I might open my heart. . . . But God is here, Who not only has compassion, but can save to the uttermost. . .*[2]

Two days later he wrote:

> *Oh, what a load is a barren heart. I feel a little forlorn pleasure in thinking over the time that is past and drown some of my heaviness by writing to my friends in England. . .*[3]

Dolly attacked him constantly in the home now. On February 6 he noted:

> *I sometimes walk in my garden and try to pray to God, and if I pray at all, it is in the solitude of a walk. I thought my soul a little. . .(better) today, but soon gross darkness returned; spoke a word or two to a. . .[Muslim] upon the things of God, but I feel as bad as they. . .*[4]

Life did not improve for William. He could escape his

misery during the day by attending the indigo plant, although his spirit was still low. Then at night he had to return to the source of his misery. He didn't want to remember how Andrew Fuller's wife had gone insane in 1792. She had gone mad after a child died too. But what was William thinking? Was Dolly insane? In March he dug out two books he had brought to India with him. Never had he imagined he would be reading them because of someone in his own family. The books were written by an acquaintance in Leicester, Dr. Arnold. The volumes were titled *Observations on the Nature, Kinds, Causes, and Preventions of Insanity.*

"Good heavens," gasped William after reading awhile, "Dolly may actually be insane!" Later he wrote in his journal that his "soul was overwhelmed with depression."

Finally Thomas and his wife came to visit him.

"Oh, how I've longed to seek advice on this matter," William told Thomas privately.

And he related to Thomas the many occurrences of Dolly's suspicions about his infidelity. The usually impulsive, exuberant Thomas was cautiously noncommittal. Did he suspect William of being crazy? At dinner Dolly was at her absolute best. She was witty, optimistic, and completely coherent. Thomas appeared uncomfortable as he watched her. And Mrs. Thomas was not watching Dolly so much as she was watching William! Had Dolly talked to her about her suspicions? Did Mrs. Thomas think William was at fault? The dinner scene was almost diabolical in its unspoken suspicions.

And yet at bedtime Dolly was angry. "I saw the way you looked at Mrs. Thomas. And I saw the way she looked at you. Old friends, are you?"

The next day Thomas was subdued. It was as if he were

weighing the facts. Either conclusion must have been incredible to him. Was Dolly insane to some degree? Or was mild-mannered William an insatiable womanizer? Or just crazy? Thomas looked more and more wretched, trying to decide which was the case. The solution seemed beyond reach.

"I'm going for a walk," he told William. "Alone."

In the home William sat at the dining table with Dolly and Mrs. Thomas. Mrs. Thomas was not looking at him with approval. In fact he had never seen her so sour.

"Perhaps I should go to the warehouse," he said uncomfortably. "We are sending out a shipment of indigo soon."

"Perhaps you should," said Mrs. Thomas dryly.

"You approve, do you?" snapped Dolly, staring hatefully at Mrs. Thomas. "So you can discreetly slip out a few minutes later and join him?"

After that moment Thomas and his wife no longer doubted William. Now Thomas discussed the situation in full with him. Thomas also consulted Arnold's books. He did not agree with William's assessment that Dolly had a form of insanity termed "ideal" by Arnold, an insanity in which a person perceives things that do not exist. Thomas believed Dolly had Arnold's "notional" insanity. In that form the person distorts reality. Specifically, Thomas said, Dolly took one passion to an extreme: the passion of jealousy.

"But we could argue about classification endlessly with no merit," said Thomas. "The immediate necessity is what do we do about it?"

"We don't tell anyone," cautioned William.

"No, of course not. She may come out of it. Perhaps it is Peter's death and her own grating illnesses that have temporarily robbed her senses. We shall pray."

But several weeks later it was clear only that Dolly had further deteriorated. She now followed William out of the house every day, insisting that he was visiting women. She screamed accusations at him in public. She now threatened his life in the house, often brandishing a kitchen knife. In June he wrote in his journal:

> *I have had very sore trials in my own family from a quarter which I forbear to mention. Have greater need for faith and patience than ever I had and I bless God that I have not been altogether without supplies of these graces from God tho[ugh] alas I have much to complain from within. . .*[5]

William set his journal aside. It was unbearable to write again and again of his heartache. He had much to be thankful for, yet he was in the depths of despair. What must God think of his weakness? Would he ever write in his journal again? Perhaps not. Suddenly Thomas and his wife were back in Mudnabati. Usually Dolly remained very stable in front of Thomas, but this time she forgot herself at dinner and attacked William. She battered his head and scratched at his face.

"You scoundrel!" she screamed. "You rogue!"

Just as abruptly she calmed and began eating. William was torn apart inside. Dolly's condition was heartbreaking, yet in spite of his agony it comforted him that other people knew beyond any doubt that it was Dolly who was insane, not him.

Thomas was downcast when he met privately with William

later. "This cannot continue, William. Your boys are being poisoned. And you have no possibility of spreading the Gospel under such conditions. She follows you into the open. In fact, the natives will think you are a demon or something."

"I'm so glad you are here," said William. "I wasn't even expecting you."

"Do you know why I came?" Thomas pulled a letter from inside his coat. "Dolly sent me this letter express. It is full of falsehoods about your infidelity, William." He put his hand on William's shoulder. "I myself should become violent under such unjust attacks. But God gave you this affliction, William, because you of all people can bear it. What other person could answer her charges with unimpeachable conduct? Yes, you can bear it. I'm sure of it."

"But what can we do?"

"I've sent for the Udnys. We will all counsel Dolly."

After the Udnys arrived the two couples did counsel Dolly for hours and hours. Dolly's madness was baffling. She was remarkably sane on any subject but William. Then she made one outrageous accusation after another against him. They tried another tack. Letters from England had finally begun to arrive, after almost two years. So they read Dolly the letters and discussed them. Perhaps letters from home would ground her, pacify her. They read her the letters from the Carey and Plackett families. They read her letters from old friends in Moulton and Leicester. Some of the letters had wonderful news. The churches in the association were prospering as never before. Much of the growth was attributed to the Careys. Their mission was the talk of the English Midlands. And London was coming alive for missionary work. There would almost certainly be a London Mission Society organized. And this too was spurred by the talk of the Careys.

"And what did you think of the odd turns of the French Revolution?" continued George Udny. "Good heavens, the rebels have actually banned Christian churches and announced the glorious revolution's new church: the Church of Reason!"

Dolly laughed softly to acknowledge the absurdity of it. But no. The letters did not pacify her. She could discuss a letter's contents in the most rational terms, then launch an attack on William in the next breath.

Afterwards Thomas took William aside. "I think we have only one alternative, William. . ."

"Wait," cautioned William and told of a startling development. Dolly was pregnant again. She was expecting a child the following January.

"Yes. We'll wait then," said Thomas. "Sometimes childbirth itself has been known to be a cure for mental illness. Dr. Arnold agrees to that assertion in his books."

One letter from England had been withheld from Dolly. It caused William much anguish. It came from the mission society. The letter repeated scathing criticism from some London clerics about William getting involved in a moneymaking scheme and abandoning his mission. Then in a softer tone William's own society admonished him. Oh, how the letter stung William. His only consolation was that Andrew Fuller had probably not known about the letter, himself being very sick at the time. William wrote the society immediately explaining his labor in India would speak for him. He reassured them the indigo business only financed his missionary efforts. He himself was poor and always would be—until the

Gospel was published in both Bengali and Hindi!

"If only they knew," he lamented. "But even this letter they won't read for many months."

So all through 1795 William suffered under the weight of the society's admonishment and Dolly's tantrums. That fall his frustration burst forth for the first time in a letter to his sisters:

> *(Dolly's) misery and rage is extreme; (English and other) Europeans have repeatedly talked to her, but in vain; and what may be the end of all God alone knows. Bless God all the dirt which she throws is such as cannot stick; but it is the ruin of my children to hear such continual accusations. . .*[6]

So at last, his family in England knew. Later, Thomas wrote Andrew Fuller about Dolly's condition. The society had to be informed. And it was best done by a physician. Thomas held nothing back. He described her attacks on William, her threats, her profane accusations. He ended the letter on a note of optimism. In January she would give birth to a baby. Perhaps she might recover. But William knew that Andrew Fuller himself once held that hope. His own very disturbed wife had given birth to a child, then gone completely insane, followed soon by her death!

 eleven

D uring Dolly's pregnancy William had to pursue his work. He had learned by now that the indigo plant required close supervision only the three months of the summer rainy season. During the rest of the year, especially the winter months of November to February, he was free to visit villages in his indigo-growing "district," which covered four hundred square miles and enveloped two hundred villages. He resolved to cover half his district every winter. The water receded in this season, so William could work his way about the countryside, often walking on ridges between the watery fields. When the water was very low he rode his horse. He would enter a village, do his business, then artfully begin a discussion with a handful of people. The number of Indians, ever open and curious, would grow. And soon William would be delivering the Gospel.

"My sentence structure is still English and I am still lacking their idioms," he told Thomas, "but they complain so much about the anguish I cause their souls I am sure they get the idea."

William still found time to work on his translations with Ram Ram Basu or his other pundit. Often he labored into the night, in the murky light of a mustard oil lamp, quill pen in hand. Sundays he always preached in Mudnabati, both to Indians in the open and to the Europeans in the lower floor of the house. On November 1, 1795, William officially chartered a Baptist Church in Mudnabati. The Thomases were there with Samuel Powell, whom William baptized.

Dolly was being managed. Servants watched her carefully for any sign of violence. She did not abuse the servants or the boys, but spoke against William constantly. Much of the time he was far away in some village. In her last months of pregnancy she was not as anxious to follow William when he left the house. In January of 1796 William was at Mudnabati to assist the birth of their baby boy. They named this boy Jonathan. Felix was now ten, Willy, five, and Jabez, two. William, and the Thomases too, watched anxiously to see if Dolly improved. When the infant Johnny was sleeping she seemed to focus on William again. She had not improved. She was worse. The Thomases witnessed Dolly lunge at William with a knife!

"Confinement," said Thomas sternly. "It's the only way to keep yourself safe, William."

"I must think long and hard about that."

"No," objected Thomas glumly, "you must do it now. Think of the boys' fates if you were incapacitated."

And so in early 1796 Dolly was confined to her room with Jonathan. She had books to read. Sewing and writing materials were also provided. Thomas, who seemed most able to calm her, explained to her that she could gain her full freedom again. She did not even have to accept the fact that William was faithful. All she had to do was control her jealousy. On the other hand if she tried to escape the room to continue her vendetta against William she would have even less freedom. He explained how she could be shackled to the bed, hands and feet.

"Fetter William," she replied, "so he can't visit his women."

In the evenings William still translated the Bible into Bengali, often with Dolly screaming in her room and the boys scrapping nearby. The boys were very undisciplined now, with no mother and virtually no father to reprimand them. How could William reprimand them when they suffered such turmoil from parents who should have protected them? And his time was so limited too. Was this translating not God's plan for him? So he worked as the boys fought and argued. He consulted Ram Ram Basu constantly. How he wished he could convert his pundit. William had been in India almost three years now and had not made one official convert. He knew Ram Ram Basu understood the Gospel. Why did he reject it? Then in the summer William was shocked to hear Ram Ram Basu accused of adultery. And the charge turned out to be true!

"How is it possible?" agonized William. "This is the very same Ram Ram Basu who composed our first hymn in Bengali with the words: 'Oh who, save Jesus, can deliver us from the eternal darkness of sin?' "

Other things came to light about Ram Ram Basu. In his clerk's job he had been dishonest too. He was little better than a common embezzler. Oh, how William hated to let him go. But let him go, he did. The mission must at all times be blameless. The native school William had started also suffered because its teacher, a friend of Ram Ram Basu, quit in a huff.

"How much more disappointment can I endure?" lamented William, thinking of Dolly and Ram Ram Basu. "But what foolishness am I indulging? Haven't I translated the Book of Job? Did I learn nothing?"

He went back to work. He soon had a teacher again for the

school. About thirty Indians attended, some as young as five, some as old as twenty. They were all castes. A few were orphans, who required food and lodging. William hired yet another pundit, this one younger than Ram Ram Basu and much more poetic. It was not long before he was writing John Ryland in a letter that besides Bengali he was now conversant in Hindi, the language spoken by the natives all the way west from Bengal. William didn't mention he also studied Sanskrit, the Indian equivalent of the western world's Latin. Sanskrit would unlock much of India's classic literature and sacred Scriptures. But William knew many of the clerics back in England disapproved of studying the native holy works.

"But I see it as a treasure chest that will improve my translation of the Bible into India's idioms and tongues," he insisted to his pundits, who could not have agreed more.

One boost to his nighttime studies was the gift of bright candles from a new friend in the town of Dinajpur. The benefactor's name was Ignatius Fernandez, a Portuguese Macaoan by birth. He owned a candle factory. It was the effervescent Thomas who led him back into Christianity. When Fernandez learned of William's work he sent him bright-burning candles as well as money to buy reference books. No longer did William squint at night under the dim light cast by a mustard oil lamp.

"Help comes from out of the blue," marveled William. "But of course it is God who provides."

Then one day in October a young Englishman walked into Mudnabati. He was John Fountain, there to help William! William had not even known about him. Fountain arrived before the mission society's letter could announce his arrival.

He was of course a Baptist, but also a Midlander like William. He loved music and was anxious to begin helping. Fountain was set up in his own bungalow a quarter of a mile away. A fanatic about bathing, he soon had William plunging into the Tangan River every morning too.

William's spirits never rose too high because Dolly's misery was ever present. By the early spring of 1797 in a letter to Andrew Fuller he lamented:

> *My family trials. . .continue and increase. Some attempts on my life have been made but I hope nothing of that kind is to be found now. God has graciously preserved me, and given me that support that I have not been remarkably retarded in my public work thereby. I am sorely distressed to see my dear children before whom the greatest indecencies and most shocking expressions of rage are constantly uttered and who are constantly taught to hate their father; tis true they don't regard what is said, yet it invariably imbues their minds with a kind of brutish ferocity, and lownishness which to me is very distressing. . .*[1]

Yet, as he modestly implied in the letter, his public work progressed. He was acutely aware of what deviltry his mistakes in translating the Bible into Indian vernaculars could lead to. With God always in mind he was very meticulous. He tested his translation into Bengali again and again off his pundit. The pundit critiqued his style and syntax. Also the pundit read the translation and explained its content to William. In this way William tested its faithfulness to the

Bible. By the spring of 1797 he had revised Thomas's work on Matthew, Mark, Luke, and James and translated the rest of the New Testament.

"The entire New Testament in Bengali!" raved George Udny. "What an achievement."

"But it's not in print yet," replied William in a worried tone. "Printing will be very expensive. No type is produced in India, and the typemakers in England do not produce type with the Bengali alphabet. If we order such type made and purchase a press from England I've calculated that to print a few thousand copies it will cost thousands—not rupees, Mr. Udny, but English pounds!"

"For heaven's sakes, William. Let it rest. You must take a break before the indigo season starts."

A break? Who had time for a break? Still, at Udny's urging William took a second trip to Bhutan with Thomas. William discovered Thomas needed a break too. He had never seen him so discouraged. Thomas confided that he might move to Calcutta and resume his practice of medicine. His inability to convert any heathens to Christ weighed on him heavily. Why were conversions so soul-wrenchingly difficult?

William tried to bolster his spirits, "What could a minister do even in England, friend, if it were as dark and rude again as when Julius Caesar discovered it? And suppose one had to learn English so as to talk to the natives? And then suppose that one had no Holy Scriptures in English but could spread the Gospel only by preaching?"

"Perhaps so," commented Thomas.

Thomas perked up but then admitted he was deep in debt again. He acted his normal exuberant self as the two exchanged gifts with Sri Naya, the suba. They gave the suba a compass and a mirror. He overwhelmed them in return: swords, helmets, shields, and embroidered cloth. The lamas, or priests, were not friendly this time. They heard the suba discussing with these two outsiders a mission in their midst. They watched their suba imitate the manners of the outsiders. Finally the head priest could stand it no longer. He questioned Thomas and William about their customs in such anger that the suba had to send him away. The two men had indeed contemplated with George Udny a mission in Bhutan. But Bhutan was a ticklish situation. As pleasant as the country seemed, it was not under the rule of the East India Company. The Bhutans might think the missionaries were spies preparing the way for a British takeover. On the other hand, the British authorities might see them as missionaries out of control.

When the two men parted to go to their separate indigo plantations Thomas simply said, "I must leave Mahipaldighi and go to Calcutta, brother."

And so the mercurial Thomas was gone. Udny gave his job at Mahipaldighi to a good man, Samuel Powell. William prayed for both of them and their families, but he had little time to worry about the fate of Thomas or Powell. The indigo season was starting. First, he had to send William Roxburgh, his botanist colleague in Calcutta, twenty-four kinds of plants he had meticulously collected in Bhutan. And then William had all his evangelical work among the villages to continue too. And he had to persevere at his unique gift from God: his translations.

"The major question now is: How do we get our New Testament in Bengali printed?" he asked John Fountain.

How he longed to order type and a press from England.

Improvements had recently been made in printing presses. It was rumored all-metal presses would soon be the norm. And levers would replace the great screws to press the platen with its paper against the typefaces. Not that William would be able to purchase the new equipment, but wouldn't many older wooden screw presses become available?

"If only I didn't have to order the type from England," he lamented, all the while longing for the wonderful modern type designed by John Baskerville of London.

Type came in one-inch slivers that were set by hand into a form. Most presses printed not just one page from the form but at least two pages. The type was inked and a platen was screwed up to press a sheet of paper against the type. A good press had springs that made the process quicker, but the best printer could impress only about two hundred sheets of paper in one hour. How many days would it take to produce one New Testament?

"Oh, I must stop thinking about it," William told himself. "It will slow down my mastery of Hindi and my translation of the Old Testament into Bengali."

As always, Dolly concerned him too. She was not improving. He resisted shackling her, but she did nothing to deserve the freedom she had. Locked in her room she ranted from morning until night. What would happen if the poor woman ever decided to reverse her hours? How would he ever sleep? Worse yet, what would happen if she escaped her room? She had already attacked him several times. But it was her effect on the boys that really worried him.

One day in December a beaming George Udny approached William. "I've just learned Calcutta is getting a type foundry!"

"For Bengali type?" asked William breathlessly.

"Yes. They will make type for all the vernaculars of India!"

William was stunned by God's provision. "So now we must keep our eyes and ears open for a used press."

"And a printer," added Udny.

So William waited and worked. By now he had a regular group of correspondents in England. He was candid about everything and everyone in Mudnabati but Dolly. It was only to Andrew Fuller and his sisters that he was completely candid. To all others, even his father and brother, his comments were guarded. In January of 1798 William wrote Polly and her caretaker Ann:

> *Poor Mrs. C. is as wretched as insanity can make her almost and often makes all family so too. But we are supported by a gracious God. . .*[2]

The summer of 1798 was traumatic. One day in July William traveled across his four-hundred-square-mile dominion, pleased with green fields bursting with rice, hemp, and the precious indigo. Ten days of rain later, his dominion was a vast lake. Even beyond the old river channels some of the fields were under water as deep as twenty feet!

"This season's crop is totally destroyed," said George Udny. "I may have to give up indigo just as Thomas did," he added. "The East India Company expects profits, not excuses."

William was shocked by Udny's pessimism. Give up indigo? "The area north is higher," he countered, "less prone to flooding."

"I'll loan you money to get started if you want to try it there." Abruptly Udny smiled. "I'm so downcast, William, I forgot to tell you I've located a press in Calcutta."

"A press!" William was so grateful, but was afraid to ask its cost.

"You may forget its cost," said Udny, anticipating his dilemma. "It's my gift to your mission."

"Bless you. You are our best benefactor."

In September the press and type arrived by boat. It was not long before William and John Fountain had the press set up. The natives began calling the huge wooden press the "sahibs' idol," an irony appreciated by both William and Fountain. Setting type and printing were acquired skills. Progress was remarkably slow. But their efforts seemed inconsequential compared to events in Europe.

The French Revolution was collapsing, creating opportunities for the ambitious. A young French general named Napoleon conquered northern Italy and was said to have designs on Egypt. Was this budding tyrant a threat to Britain's crown jewel, India? England would not wait to find out. Peaceful Sir John Shore, reader of Persian and Sanskrit, was no longer the man to be governor of the East India Company. The year 1797 had brought the three Wellesley brothers to India. Richard was the new governor. Brother Henry was his personal secretary. Brother Arthur was Richard's military arm.

"We are into a new era in India," cautioned George Udny. "The Wellesleys will use the French militarism as an excuse to dominate India. The thing I fear most is Arthur Wellesley's attitude toward evangelism. I fear he will not remain benign as did our erudite Claphamite, Sir John Shore."

By 1799 it was obvious the Wellesleys were going to subdue the last of India's native strongmen—in the name of protecting India from France. In Mysore a sultan named Tipu ruled. An enormous British army was being raised to attack him.

Still William labored on. Despite the encouragement he had tried to give Thomas in Bhutan, William himself was at times profoundly depressed. The printing took far too much time. And he had not made one convert yet. He could not even convert his own pundits. How was it possible that they knew the Gospel and still rejected it? He wrote his frustration to members of the Society:

> *I am almost grown callous, and am tempted to preach as if their hearts were invulnerable. But this dishonors the grace and power of God, Who has promised to be with His ministers to the end; and it destroys all energy, and makes preaching stupidly formal. . .*[3]

Oh, what a weak instrument he was, as he described himself in a letter to venerable John Newton. But he plodded after duty. In the spring of 1799 William journeyed to Calcutta to visit Kitty. Her husband Charles Short was gravely ill. After giving what comfort he could to the Shorts he visited Thomas and acquired printing supplies before heading back to Mudnabati by boat. He was very troubled by what he saw all along the rivers. On ghats, the steps or ramps that led down to the river, he saw helpless people abandoned. The old and sick were simply left to starve to death!

And those were not the only barbaric things he saw. At Noaserai, about thirty miles north of Calcutta, a crowd was gathered in the evening gloom at the side of the Hooghly River. A suspicious William had his boatman stop.

"What is the occasion?" he asked in Bengali.

"We are witnessing a great act of holiness," was the answer.

Then William saw a man's body stretched out on a stack of wood. The wood was piled about three feet high. Milling about the dead man were men and women in their best silken clothes. One woman stood motionless beside the body. A chill swept over William. He had heard of the terrible Hindu practice called "sati," but had refused to believe it.

"Is that woman the man's widow?" he asked suspiciously.

"Yes."

"Is she going to die with her husband?"

"Yes."

"Is she willing?"

"Of course she is. It is great act of holiness."

William was now as angry as he had ever been in his life. "No!" He tried to reach the woman. The crowd blocked him. "You must not do this!" he screamed in Bengali. "It's murder!"

The calmness evaporated. A woman took the widow by the elbow and hurried her around the funeral pyre. The widow carried a plate of sweets called "thioy," which she threw to the crowd. She circled the pyre six times in all. William protested loudly. The onlookers became very angry with him. Only their fear of the English authorities protected him.

"Stop, in the name of justice!" yelled William.

"Oh, go away if you don't like it!" growled the onlookers.

"No. I will witness this murder!" answered William, hoping to frighten them of impending punishment.

But the woman mounted the pyre and lay down beside her husband. Was she calm in her "holy" act or petrified with fear? William could not break though the crowd. The whole scene seemed too incredible to fathom. It could not be happening. Finally leaves were piled high on top of both bodies.

A vat of butter was poured on top of that. Then four men pressed down the pile with two bamboo poles.

"I see that!" screamed William. "You won't let her get up, will you?"

But who could hear him? The crowd was screaming with earsplitting fervor and dancing about with joy. Suddenly the pyre burst into flames. If the woman screamed in agony no one would have heard her. William stumbled back into the boat, his soul seared forever by the sight. All the way back to Mudnabati he thought of *sati* and the abandonment of the old and the diseased on the ghats. There were other practices like sacrificing babies to the river he had refused to believe too. But now he had to wonder if those abominations were also true.

How could he ever have considered himself useless? Enraged by the injustices all around him he now wrote:

> *I would not abandon the Mission for all the fellowships and finest spheres in England. My greatest calamity would be separation from this service. May I be useful in laying the foundations of Christ's Church in India; I desire no greater reward, nor can conceive higher honor. The work, to which God has set His hands, will infallibly prosper. Christ has begun to besiege this ancient and strong fortress, and will assuredly carry it. It is not His way to desert what He has once undertaken. . .*[4]

Back in his district he once again was confronted by problems with the indigo. This year it was not a flood that ruined the crop but a drought. The riverine world was drying up. In May of 1799, George Udny came to see him.

"I'm sorry, William, but I can't support you here past August. What have you decided to do?"

"I must think more on it."

It stung him to his heart's core to think of leaving Peter behind. But Mudnabati was finished. Should he start another plantation to the north? Or should he find something in Calcutta? In his blackest moments he thought of returning to England. Weren't five years, his wife's sanity, and his son enough sacrifice for India? What should he do?

Then William was startled by a letter from England.

twelve

/ t was May of 1799. The letter, dated October of the previous year, was from a William Ward:

Dear Mr. Carey,

I know not whether you will remember a young man, a printer, walking with you from Rippon's Chapel one Sunday, and conversing with you on your journey to India. But that person is coming to see you, and writes this happy letter. His services were accepted by the Society on the 16th. It was a happy meeting. The missionary spirit was all alive . . . . Sometime in the spring I hope to embark with the others. . .[1]

Others? And Ward, a printer? William was stunned, then ebullient. Surely this was a directive from God: Keep up the good fight! He seemed to recall Ward now. Ward was about thirty, a friend to Andrew Fuller and some others in the Baptist association. He was very outspoken, so much so he had been jailed a time or two. Still, he was a printer! Days later William learned eight missionaries were coming. Besides Ward and three married couples there was Miss Tidd, John Fountain's fiancée. William immediately began to plan another indigo plantation farther north. He had no time to waste now. Staked by a loan from George Udny, just as he had promised, William made a down payment on a plantation in the north. In the meantime he would translate as he awaited the arrival of the missionaries.

"Then we will move lock, stock, and barrel to the new plantation."

In October he received word from George Udny that the missionaries had arrived. They numbered not only eight adults but five children too. But there were difficulties. This new governor Richard Wellesley was no easygoing Sir John Shore. Even though the missionaries had sailed aboard the American ship *Criterion* and disembarked at Serampore, a Danish settlement several miles upriver from Calcutta, the British authorities were threatening them. John Fountain, very anxious to greet his fiancée, rushed to Serampore. By December 1, 1799, he returned to Mudnabati a married man, although he brought not his bride back with him, but William Ward.

"We bear very sad news," said Ward in William's study, startled as Dolly screamed from her room. But Fountain must have briefed him well because he quickly continued, "One of our companions, Mr. Grant, died of a fever within days after our arrival."

"That fast?" gasped William. "It could only have been cholera. God rest his soul." He lapsed into silence, never expecting such grim news. Finally he continued, "And what do the British authorities say about your travel?"

"We can't travel at all," answered Ward. "They are adamant."

William was almost too puzzled to speak. "And yet, Mr. Ward, here you are."

"Serampore is run by a good man," explained John Fountain. "Colonel Bie issued Ward a Danish passport."

"Yes," agreed William. "The old colonel is a fine man."

John Fountain cleared his throat. "Colonel Bie has offered the missionaries permanent asylum in Serampore. He has offered us his own governor's mansion as a church on Sunday. He will also provide a school building if we wish. And as you can see by the presence of William Ward, Danish passports enable missionaries to travel around—at least, briefly —in British territory."

Ward interrupted eagerly, "And the colonel says we can set up a press there in Serampore. He will in no way interfere with our printing! I hear the New Testament is almost ready to print."

William waved at sheaves of paper. "Except for a few minor chapters of the Old Testament the entire Bible is ready, friend."

"The entire Bible into Bengali?" asked Ward in amazement. "You've done the impossible!"

William smiled. " 'I can do all things through Christ which strengtheneth me.' "

"Philippians 4:13, of course," reflected Ward. "Well, what is it to be then, Mr. Carey? Are you coming to Serampore?"

William's mind was reeling. He would lose hundreds of pounds he had already invested in the new indigo plantation to the north. What a crushing loss that would be. And these young missionaries seemed oblivious to the fact that brave German Moravians, missionaries almost without peer, had utterly failed at Serampore after fifteen years of toil. And yet the new missionaries from England were trapped in Serampore.

"God's will seems clear," William finally said.

Next morning John Fountain rushed back to Serampore

but Ward stayed to help the Careys move. A few days later when George Udny came to visit him he was stunned by William's change of direction.

"This is astonishing," said Udny. "I came here to tell you that I'm being transferred to Calcutta to sit on the Supreme Council and to warn you that my successor despises missionaries. Not only that, good friend, but I've learned Richard Wellesley will soon allow no printing in British territory outside Calcutta. And now I discover our God has already directed you to a safe haven in Serampore!"

By January 1, 1800, the boats were loaded. It seemed appropriate for the new century that there was an enormous amount to transfer to Serampore. The press, the manuscripts, the four boys, and Dolly were the most precious cargo. But William also had hundreds of botanical cuttings he had to take with him. He had never neglected his botany. It was as natural as breathing. Tending to a plant was a breath of fresh air. Besides son Peter, the garden he left behind saddened William the most. On the other hand he could now frequently see his correspondent William Roxburgh, who headed the Calcutta Botanic Gardens. He had another close correspondent there too: Judge Colebrooke, the only Englishman in India who knew more Sanskrit than William.

"I made not one convert," William sighed to Ward as he watched Mudnabati disappear below the horizon. "And yet God let me translate the entire Bible into Bengali, and learn both Hindi and Sanskrit. Do you think He is telling me something?"

Dolly behaved admirably all the way down the river. Was she getting better? "What a great blessing that would be for the family," prayed William. Even with so much more cargo the trip was easier than their journey to Mudnabati five years earlier because now the mighty rivers swept them along toward the sea. On January 10 the boats wound their way through a maze of sailing ships unloading and loading cargo at a busy, prosperous village on the west bank. It was Serampore. Visible far to the south was Calcutta. Across the Hooghly on the east bank was the British garrison at Barrackpore. William was told Richard Wellesley, the governor, spent his weekends there, reaching it from Calcutta by a ship of the Crown.

"No wonder the governor was well aware of the recent arrival of the missionaries," noted William.

The Careys were welcomed warmly by the other missionaries. John Fountain was with his excitable young bride, formerly Miss Tidd. The David Brunsdons were also a very young couple. The Marshmans were older, both in their early thirties like Ward. Joshua Marshman was an experienced schoolteacher and protégé of John Ryland. His pugnacious look matched his reputation for being a fiery debater. But he was well mannered, a gracious host. He would, William suspected, organize their schools to a new level as well as tackle problems once handled by Thomas. Joshua's wife Hannah looked sturdy and industrious. Her stern look at the four rowdy Carey boys told William they might soon get some discipline he hadn't the heart to give them.

William visited Mrs. Grant to give his condolences. "And don't worry, madam," he concluded, "we will care for you and your children as if you are our own."

Without hesitation he purchased a very large house on two acres. All the missionaries would live in it and share a common dining room. The acreage would allow a splendid garden. The first year of the new century would be a year for forming a strong communal settlement. There were now five men, five women, and nine children. More than ever they must fuse into a fellowship. Perhaps it was helpful too that John Thomas was not there. That way the others looked for leadership from the one man experienced in India: William. Yet he disdained the mantle of "headman." Their union was going to be a patriarchy. Every adult male had a say but the majority opinion ruled. Leadership would rotate monthly. Duties included purchase of supplies, chairing meetings, keeping accounts, supervising servants, interviewing callers and conducting church services.

"We have only one master: Christ," insisted William.

All earnings were pooled for the fellowship. A major source of income would be from boarding schools for both boys and girls. Each family in the fellowship was apportioned what it needed from the pool of earnings. All surpluses were used to expand the mission. Their two main priorities were established early. The way had to be prepared for the publication of the Bible in Bengali. And the buildings must be built in which the Marshmans would promote their boarding schools, including a free school for all poor children, Indian or otherwise.

The new arrivals were a godsend to William. Joshua Marshman was not only their best diplomat but picked up Bengali at lightning speed. Hannah virtually took over the Carey boys. She would not tolerate their rotten behavior. Soon they began to display some manners. Most surprising of all was Ward's influence on the boys. Felix and Willy became so attached to Ward that they were soon usefully employed at the press.

"And Colonel Bie, the governor of Serampore, keeps his

word in every respect," said William, overcome by how well this change of direction from Mudnabati prospered.

Colonel Bie's mansion was open every Sunday for their church service. He urged the Danes to send their children to the schools run by the Marshmans. He paid Ward to do all his government printing. He insisted he would buy the first Bengali Bible printed. In March he feted the missionaries with a formal dinner. The ladies were delivered to the mansion in litters. The lavish dinner lasted two hours. The governor himself was seventy-two and very temperate. He rose every morning at five to take a long walk.

In April when the missionaries observed an entire day of Thanksgiving they had a surprise visitor. "John Thomas!" exclaimed William.

Yet Thomas looked unhinged. His activities were more desperate than ever. William suspected he might even be involved in the rum trade. But the most disturbing thing were signs of mental illness. Thomas had a vacant look in his eyes. With his heart aching William vowed to watch him closely. But soon Thomas was gone again.

By May the missionaries printed the first page of the Bengali Bible. The first step of their method of printing was for William and Fountain to prepare clear, errorless copy of the manuscript. Then Ward and Brunsdon, aided by Felix and Willy, would set the type and print the pages. They even now employed an Indian named Panchana, who was a metalsmith so skilled he could make type. Such all-pervading progress seemed too fortunate to William. And it was. Dolly's condition, improved at first arrival, worsened so much she could no longer socialize with the others. At one meal she had attacked Ward.

"You beat my children, don't you?" she raged.

William's infidelity was no longer her main delusion. Her accusations now usually stemmed from anxiety over the children. She was either fearful about them or in a rage. She seemed to possess no other emotions. Her anxieties were unfounded. In fact, Felix and Willy had been led back to Christ by the counseling of Ward. The three even read the Bible together. Felix, who in Mudnabati had shunned the Bible, often went out with the men into the villages when they evangelized. But Ward and the others had been prepared for Dolly's relapse and her terrible rage. Her sister Kitty had not. She had come to visit Dolly when the Careys first arrived in Serampore. Dolly was acting almost normal then. When Kitty returned in June Dolly was lost again. Kitty sat dejectedly in William's study while Dolly ranted in her nearby room.

Kitty sighed, "My poor sister is stark mad just as you say."

William seemed never in a hurry but always busy doing something. That same June he sent the botanist Roxburgh in Calcutta a list of the 427 species of plants he tended in his new garden! He requested from Roxburgh 66 more! Once, Marshman scolded William for not protecting himself in the merciless summer sun as he tended his garden.

William, tenderly holding a sprout, teased Marshman, "My good sir, you only appreciate a garden as an ox does grass." It was a rare moment of humor for William. Events always seemed so sobering. In August John Fountain became feverish and died with stunning quickness. His young wife was pregnant. The missionaries mourned his sudden death. Hindus, especially the highest caste Brahmins, now taunted them in their evangelical outings: Why would your God kill two of his messengers in the very first year? But the missionaries fought back.

Even mild-tempered William chided the Brahmins. "Did that wooden idol make you Brahmins or did you Brahmins make it?" he asked, waving at a statue of the goddess Kali.

Sometimes William would sway even the Brahmins with his great knowledge of their sacred writings. "You have read the Shastras yourself?" they would ask in amazement. "We have never seen them ourselves." And yet, later the Indians would throw stones at him. Still, although William preached three or four times on Sunday, often he went into the villages to preach Friday too. All the men preached. William thought Ward, when he mastered Bengali, might become the most persuasive of them all. And on October 21 Felix preached for the first time in a village.

William was overjoyed. "I have more cause for joy than anyone. . ." Ward had truly saved Felix.

The Serampore Mission began printing religious tracts in Bengali. The men would hand out the tracts and urge their listeners to read them or to take them to someone in their village who could read it for them. Ward was ecstatic. "God has given me, a man less than the least of all saints, the grace that I should print for the heathens the unsearchable riches of Christ!"

In late November Governor Bie asked William to teach English to a relative of his, a lady named Charlotte Rumohr. She came from Schleswig, an area sometimes German, sometimes Danish. She was a tiny unmarried woman the same age as William. Much of her life she had spent as an invalid, unable to speak or walk. Her recent retreat into the tropics had rejuvenated her. She now spoke and even walked a little. William could not help thinking of his own sister Polly, also paralyzed and mute. Polly had a heart as large as a mountain, so he was very sympathetic to tiny Charlotte Rumohr.

"She is so bright," he told Colonel Bie later, "she will be speaking English in only a few weeks."

Meanwhile a great event seemed on the horizon at the mission. John Thomas had been summoned to set the dislocated shoulder of a Hindu carpenter named Krishna Pal. Thomas was still not well in William's opinion, but somehow he appealed very strongly to Krishna Pal. Krishna, about thirty-five, began to visit the mission often. Not only Thomas but Felix gave him spiritual advice. They wanted to convert him, their job made no easier by their own decision to make any convert abandon his caste. And they also made Krishna Pal go back and tell his wife and daughter exactly what he was considering. His neighbors threatened him when they learned what he was doing. Nevertheless by late December it appeared Krishna Pal would at last become their first real convert. He agreed to be baptized with his advisor Felix on December 28, 1800.

"Sing, soul, sing," cried Thomas to William, "if it still can through my tears of fifteen years."

"No one deserves this more than you," said William. He was very happy for Thomas. Maybe this spiritual triumph for Christ was just the thing to stabilize his friend again.

On the Tuesday before the baptisms Ward rushed into William's study. "Come quickly. Something is wrong with John Thomas."

William could not believe his eyes when he saw Thomas. His eyes rolled wildly. He stumbled. He babbled. The men restrained him. Thomas could no more be allowed to wander about in a crazed condition than Dolly. It tore at William's heart when they had to straitjacket Thomas. The doctor's great moment of vindication was near and he was completely out of his mind!

Nevertheless, on Sunday, December 28, 1800, William gave a sermon on baptism at the governor's mansion. Then in the early afternoon all the missionaries, the governor, and dozens of onlookers gathered at the side of the Hooghly River in front of the Mission House. They sang a hymn in Bengali before William loudly explained in Bengali that the river itself was not sacred but only the act of baptism was sacred. Then he entered the Hooghly with fifteen-year-old Felix and baptized him. Then he baptized Krishna Pal, the chief attraction for dozens of Hindus on the bank.

"What a magnificent occasion," enthused Ward afterwards. "Colonel Bie was crying."

Yes, it had been magnificent, thought William, *but bizarre too*. Hindus and Muslims had been there to gawk. David Brunsdon had watched from a litter, too seriously ill to stand. Tiny Charlotte Rumohr, barely able to walk herself, had hobbled up to Krishna Pal to grab his hand and thank him. And old friend Thomas, at this great moment of triumph for his missionary work, was restrained in the schoolhouse, babbling. What a price Thomas had paid for his years in India. Still, there was hope he would recover once the excitement was over. But could the same be said for Dolly, who had been screaming rage from the Mission House?

The very next day William wrote John Sutcliffe: "Mrs. Carey is worse than ever with respect to her mental derangement."[2]

William had every reason to believe Jaymani, the sister of Krishna's wife, would be baptized in a few weeks. And who else would follow? In the meantime he had to help make arrangements for Thomas. Mrs. Thomas had been contacted by George Udny. Thomas might qualify for free treatment in the Calcutta Hospital for Lunatics because he had served the East India Company as a ship's surgeon. By January 1, 1801, Richard Wellesley himself had approved the treatment. William and Marshman escorted Thomas to the hospital.

"Get well, old friend," said William in parting.

Three weeks later William was there when they released Thomas. The doctor was calm, but still disoriented in William's opinion. Thomas was to go to Dingapore and recuperate. William felt a sense of foreboding as his old friend departed. Why would Thomas go mad just as the missionaries most prospered? Was it the excitement? For they had another high moment coming. Jaymani was baptized. Krishna Pal's wife Rasamayi seemed sure to follow. A widow named Annada seemed likely too. And in Chandernagore Krishna had three sisters very interested in Christ. He was a natural evangelist, very persuasive. He often preached to Hindu neighbors now too. William heard him.

"I too bathed in the Ganges," declared Krishna Pal. "Yes, I too worshipped dumb idols. I prostrated myself at my guru's feet. I gave gifts to the priests. I visited holy sites. I repeatedly chanted my guardian deity's name. But I found no relief from my sins. Then I heard of Jesus Christ, that He became flesh to dwell among us, that He served us, that He gave His life for my sins. What love is this? Did our gods ever show such love? Did our gods ever die for our sins? And think of this: Our gurus place their feet on our backs but Christ knelt to wash the feet of men!"

March brought another great day for the Serampore

Mission. At a special thanksgiving service William placed a bound New Testament in Bengali on the communion table. At long last it was finished. William preached a sermon on "Let the word of Christ dwell in you richly," from the book of Colossians. Marshman introduced a hymn he composed for the occasion. And the reality of the Gospel in Bengali was struck home by the presence of Krishna Pal, Jaymani, Rasamayi, and Annada, all four Bengalis now baptized Christians!

How the missionaries enjoyed distributing their New Testament. To the mission society in England they sent one hundred copies. Andrew Fuller had once said he would see that the king of England himself had a copy, just so His Majesty would see what glorious things missionaries could accomplish. Imagine! His Majesty George III holding the shoemaker's Bible. Colonel Bie, who bought the first copy, said he would send it to the king of Denmark! But it would be months before the Bibles reached that part of the world. And to dwell on their fate in high places was prideful.

April of 1801 hit William like a cyclone. Krishna Pal's thirteen-year-old daughter Golok had long been pledged to marry a Hindu named Mohan. When she tried to back out because she now considered Mohan a heathen, Hindu friends of Mohan's abducted her. Krishna was beaten up as he tried to stop the men. Golok sought protection from the authorities.

"Why should I have to swallow this poison?" she wailed.

William had to intervene. As much as he disliked his role he had to convince Golok she should honor the marriage arrangement. Couldn't she bring her husband to Christ? She reluctantly agreed to try.

On April 8, William received a note from David Brown, an

important Anglican reverend among the English in Calcutta. William had heard the Reverends Brown and Claudius Buchanan were supposed to organize a new college for Governor Wellesley in Calcutta. Apparently Wellesley was appalled at the dismal education of the young Englishmen who intended to follow their fathers into civil service in India. Such concerns by the militaristic Wellesley to create an "Oxford University of the East" were suspect to the missionaries, so Brown's letter stunned William.

"How can this be?" he gasped, and rushed to summon Marshman and Ward to his study.

thirteen

"They have offered me a position as professor of Bengali—at one thousand rupees a month!" cried William, waving the letter.

"Unsought?" asked Marshman uncertainly.

"Of course," answered William.

"Influenced by your New Testament, no doubt," added Marshman.

"But wouldn't such a position divert you from your chief purpose?" objected Ward.

"Yes," agreed William. "It might well consume much of my time. That is a drawback."

"And what are the advantages?" mulled Marshman and quickly answered himself, "One is that the income is very substantial to the mission."

"And another is that perhaps I can influence future civil servants of India. Yes, I will teach Bengali but I might just give them a reading or two from our Bengali New Testament!"

"But will Richard Wellesley approve a Nonconformist?" asked Marshman cautiously. "You know that no Nonconformists are allowed to teach at Oxford University in England."

"We will find out," said William.

Four days later Colonel Bie and Reverend Brown came to visit William. His application had been presented to Governor

161

Wellesley. Wellesley did indeed object to a Baptist. But Brown and Buchanan told him William was the very best instructor of Bengali in India, if not the world. Did not the governor want the very best for his "Oxford of the East"? So Brown and Buchanan suggested a compromise: Perhaps William could be a "tutor," not a "professor." "Only if he takes five hundred rupees a month instead of a thousand," countered Wellesley.

"I'll take five hundred," said William to the offer.

"Excellent. Do you have any more translation projects in the works?" asked Brown politely.

"You may have heard, sir, that we plan to publish the entire Bible in five volumes. Besides the New Testament volume, four volumes of the Old Testament will be published as the 'Pentateuch,' the 'Histories,' the 'Prophets,' and 'Hagiographa.' "

"Quite ambitious!" exclaimed Brown approvingly.

"Oh, that's only the beginning, God willing."

"Only the beginning?"

"We must reach all Indians. We must give the northern Indians the entire Bible in Bengali, Punjabi, and Hindi."

"Punjabi and Hindi too? But isn't that impossible?"

"And for central India we must give the entire Bible in Oriya, Marathi, and Gujarati," interrupted William.

"But surely that's impossible. . ."

"And although southern India already has the entire Bible in Tamil," continued William, "we must give them also the entire Bible in Telugu and Kanarese. You see, sir, once one has mastered Bengali, Hindi, and Sanskrit, one understands almost all the other tongues. So we will probably also translate the entire Bible into Sanskrit."

Brown looked dazed. "I'll tell my colleagues you've accepted the appointment and you seem well qualified."

Just days later, through the most incredible coincidence, British troops entered Serampore to occupy the settlement. Denmark and England were now at war. The conquest of Serampore was gentle. Colonel Bie was respected by the English. There would be no trouble. About the only result was a British officer's request that Dolly be strictly confined. On her better days she had been allowed to leave the Mission House with family for walks. But the officer had seen one of her violent outbursts. He was afraid a young soldier might overreact. Unsaid was the murder she threatened to others. William agreed to the strict confinement.

"Dolly is not taking this tighter confinement well," said William to his friends. "Now she rages more than ever."

In July David Brunsdon died of his long illness, after opinions of many physicians and applications of many remedies. Golok ran away from her husband to live at the Serampore Mission. She could no longer endure her husband's intolerance. On the other hand William found himself away from the mission more often than not. Every Tuesday he crossed the Hooghly River to ride a coach the three hours to the temporary college buildings in the center of Calcutta. There he lectured, preached, and visited colleagues until Friday afternoon. Then he journeyed back to Serampore. Almost from the first day Judge Colebrooke confided in William that he was probably going to take over Colebrooke's duties as teacher of Sanskrit. So William's future at the college looked very busy. He wasted not a minute either. Even while riding in coaches he read and translated continually.

August 17, 1801, William turned forty. It seemed a passage

from youth for him, a time to look back. He was only seven years removed from what had to be the low point of his life: the Sundarbans. He knew now the area was not only dreaded by all Bengalis for its man-eating tigers but it was also a death trap for the English and Europeans. Old friend Charles Short was dying of some insidious disease contracted there. Mudnabati, in spite of its trials, had seemed a triumph. But now these Serampore years were the pure grace of God. William had not only polished his translation of the Bible into Bengali but printed it. He enjoyed the esteem of a college teacher. He had helped establish a strong mission. His sons, finding the Way, were a source of joy now. And perhaps greatest of all: At long last the heathens were coming into the fold.

"My only pains are Dolly's agonizing madness," he told himself, "and worry for my old friend John Thomas."

In October Thomas died in Dingapore from what they said was cholera. William reflected with great sadness "who could be sure?" All he knew was that India's many diseases relentlessly claimed missionaries: son Peter, Grant, John Fountain, David Brunsdon, and now Thomas. Friend Thomas could not have been much more than forty years old himself. He had been shunned and scorned and ridiculed his last years. But William had forgiven Thomas all his idiosyncrasies long ago. Where would he be if he had not met the exuberant, optimistic Thomas? Where would the society be? Yes, Thomas was flawed. But he had a great heart. William would miss him deeply.

William certainly wasted none of the time he had in Serampore from Friday evening to Tuesday morning. He taught geography, astronomy, and natural history at the three schools for the children. As pastor he held prayer meetings and preached at the Baptist's Mission Church. As he had at Mudnabati he also oversaw a medical clinic. Illnesses varied in severity from minor infections to the dreaded leprosy. And William worked very hard with Krishna Pal's extended family and Indians in general. The Serampore Mission seemed on the verge of a great breakthrough. Nevertheless they feared that by insisting a convert must renounce his caste forever they would never attract a higher caste Hindu. But that all changed on New Year's Day, 1802. William baptized Pitambar Singh, a Hindu of the Kyast or writer's caste.

That spring William had the sad duty of executing Charles Short's will. Short had died after his long illness. William had to write Kitty, who had gone back to England. Many months later she wrote William back. Her letter conveyed great understanding. William was very grateful for Kitty. She was his bridge to the Plackett family. Her health and wit were proofs that India had not crushed Dolly but some kind of inevitability had. But it was clear now that Kitty would never return to India. Dolly was not told.

"She has more than enough to rage about," said William.

Meanwhile the conversions continued. That summer William baptized their first Muslim. And Kamalakanta, a Brahmin, now practically lived at the mission, not quite able to decide to be baptized. So it was a Brahmin named Krishna Prisad who became the first. Life was not easy for these new Christians. Their fellow Hindus and Muslims reviled them. Often, Serampore Mission was their only refuge. The war between Denmark and England ended, as did the English occupation. Serampore had been little affected. The mission work continued on.

The translators divided the labor on a New Testament in

Hindi. William was translating St. Paul's Epistles while Marshman and Ward did the Gospels. William's work at the college, now called Fort William College because that fort along the Hooghly was where it would eventually be located, gained him more esteem. To his amazement Governor Wellesley asked him to look into a rumored practice among the Hindus. Were childless women told by their priests to vow to sacrifice a baby to the sacred river if it granted them children? If so, did the women later keep their vows? Did such an abominable practice exist under the very noses of the English authorities in Calcutta? What Englishman could inquire more thoroughly than William, who now knew Bengali like a native?

"Heaven help us," lamented William, as with his usual intensity he gathered reports from around the area.

Report after report substantiated the vile practice. An area known as Ginga Saugor at the junction of the ocean and the Hooghly River was especially notorious. There mourning mothers did indeed sacrifice babies to the sacred river, often waiting for the birth of the first baby girl. Girls were not deemed as valuable as boys. Mothers gently placed the baby girls on the mud banks and left. They couldn't bear to know how the poor innocents perished. Sometimes the abandoned baby was taken by a crocodile. Sometimes it simply squirmed down into the murky river to drown. Governor Wellesley acted immediately on William's report. Such a practice was officially deemed murder!

"I now know how wonderful it is have power," said William to his fellow missionaries.

"Go after sati then!" urged Marshman.

"Yes, I will certainly make a case against that dreadful

practice of widow burning."

William threw himself into that unauthorized investigation. He gathered reports all around Calcutta to a distance of 30 miles. The total number of widows burned in that area in the last year alone was 438! He immediately submitted his report and pleaded for the governor to ban sati as murder, just as the governor had banned child sacrifice as murder. To William's consternation the government officials agreed that sati was horrible, but stressed it was a profound religious practice. And it involved willing adults, not innocent children.

"I am very disappointed," said William, "and we will continue to compile the numbers of widows burned every year and have them published. But we must not press so hard we are no longer heard."

He prayed he knew when to press the powers that be and when not to press them. "Behold, I send you forth as sheep in the midst of wolves," said the Lord, "be ye therefore wise as serpents, and harmless as doves." William was gaining influence, and he did not want to lose it because he became too much of a nuisance. In 1803 he was invited to the new Government House to present his students in a lively debate for Governor Wellesley. They debated the question: "Are Asians capable of as high a civilization as nations of the west?"

"Highly entertaining," commented the governor later. "By the way, Reverend Carey, I hear your mission society in England presented His Majesty George III your New Testament in Bengali."

"Indeed, sir!"

"The king said he was greatly pleased that his subjects should be employed in such an endeavor!"

The following year Governor Wellesley heard William's

students debate again. His brother Arthur Wellesley, fresh from several savage campaigns against the Indians in Maratha, was there too, as were all the officials of the Supreme Council and all the justices of the Supreme Court. This time William was allowed to follow the debate with a speech. He made the most of it.

"This college will obliterate our ignorance of India's languages," he predicted, "that has long hindered the power of our principles and laws, and has crippled our ministering of its energy and effect. 'Sanskrit learning,' say the Brahmins, 'is a vast forest bountiful in varied and beautiful foliage, in flowers and tender fruits.' In the past it was impenetrable behind a great thorny hedgerow. This college, by the wisdom of Lord Wellesley, will forge a highway through the hedgerow and into the forest."

"Well said," gushed Arthur Wellesley, the soldier, to William later, "and because we have finally subdued the Marathas in central India you must add their language of Marathi to your arsenal. I'll speak to Lord Wellesley about it at once."

By 1805 William was also teaching Marathi.

By that time the Serampore Mission was expanding its evangelism. The previous year had brought a wonderful surprise. Three men appeared at Serampore. They had come from the south. In 1801 Ward had left a Bengali New Testament in their village. Now they wanted to be baptized in the name of the Father, the Son, and the Holy Spirit! What power the Gospels had! In 1805 Krishna Pal and other converts accompanied the English missionaries far into the field to preach. William took Pitambar Singh to Sukh Sagar and Krishna Pal to Jessore. Ward took Krishna Pal to Debhatta, then took Krishna Prasad and Ram Ratan to Dinajpur and Mudnabati.

The missionaries went far to the north and far to the east. But not west. West took them into lands that spoke Hindi and Marathi. The missionaries were not ready for those lands yet.

The mission formalized its purpose in 1805 as the "Serampore Compact." The Serampore Compact was to be read at every mission three times a year: on the first Lord's Day in the months of January, May, and October. The compact acknowledged that no increase can come without God's grace. Their noblest example was Saint Paul, the "great champion for the glorious doctrine of free and sovereign grace." The Serampore Compact then went on to elaborate in nearly 5,000 words of text the eleven principals of the mission:

1. Missionaries must be always mindful of the infinite value of an immortal soul, so that they can stay steadfast in their goal of converting heathens.
2. They must be knowledgeable of the heathen's beliefs, so that they can understand them and refute them.
3. They must behave in an exemplary Christian way at all times.
4. They must constantly mingle with the heathens, and press for opportunities.
5. They must never forget to preach "Christ crucified." Redemption of a sinner's soul through Christ's ransom is the message.
6. They must be always accessible and courteous to the heathens.
7. They must not forget to nurture their converts in Christ. They must instruct them in their

Christian duties.

8. They must develop every talent of the heathens for usefulness and encourage Christian churches and pastors from the ranks of the natives. From that foundation they must encourage native missionaries.

9. They must translate the Holy Bible into all the native tongues of India.

10. They must encourage a life of fervent and constant prayer among themselves.

11. They must give unreservedly to these causes, never thinking of self or material things or family.

The commitment in the Serampore Compact was about as total as the missionaries could prescribe. The eleventh principal was the hardest for outsiders to accept. Yes, poverty was hard indeed. So also was denial of self. But neglect of family? "How can you deny your own family?" asked well-meaning critics. "By the very command of the Lord Himself," William could answer, remembering the Scripture that had sustained him so often, "in chapter 14 of the Book of Luke."

If any man come to me, and hate not his father, and mother, and wife, and children, and brethren, and sisters, yea, and his own life also, he cannot be my disciple.

One day in 1805 Claudius Buchanan confided to William, "The Wellesleys are being replaced." With Judge Colebrooke, Buchanan had become a strong advocate for William at the college. As vice-provost of the college he was in the main flow of information, official and unofficial. "Apparently," Buchanan continued dryly, "the directors in London are scandalized by the Wellesleys's strong-armed tactics, not to mention their extravagant use of English money and English lives."

"What will happen to the Wellesley brothers?" asked William anxiously.

"It's just like you to be concerned with them," said Buchanan. "I suspect they will be knighted and Arthur packed off to fight the French tyrant Napoleon, someone more his size. They say Napoleon has conquered Switzerland and part of Austria and now threatens all of Europe."

"Who will replace Wellesley as governor?"

"Cornwallis."

"Again?"

"Yes. The primary goal of the East India Company, after all, is money. Apparently Cornwallis governed during the most profitable years of the company's history."

Soon Cornwallis was back in India. He was towed up the Ganges River on a luxurious barge, generously restoring lands to rulers the Wellesleys had defeated. But the elderly general sickened and died, his reign lasting mere weeks. Sir George Barlow, the senior member of the Supreme Council, took over. The company was very satisfied with Barlow governing, but it was said the English Parliament did not trust him. He was too much a company insider. Nevertheless Barlow governed, as the Parliament in London was distracted by Napoleon, who showed every sign of adding Bavaria, Italy, and Poland to his "empire."

The year 1806 started pleasantly for William. He not only received the title of "professor" but his monthly salary was doubled to one thousand rupees. As an example of the kind of respect he enjoyed, all government publications in Bengali, Sanskrit, or Marathi now had to get his stamp of approval. And most exciting of all, Buchanan was now soliciting money from English officials all over India to fund not only William's translation work but that of his colleagues at Serampore.

"God has let me hit upon the key for all future translations," William confided in Buchanan. "Sanskrit. It is a 'dead' language, yet the basis for most modern Indian languages, just as the 'dead' language Latin is the basis for many modern European languages."

All the Indian pundits knew Sanskrit, so William reasoned that if he could provide them with the very best Bible in Sanskrit it would serve as the basis for all translations into modern Indian languages. It was certainly no small undertaking. The Bengali Bible, which William had labored on for ten years, still lacked the volumes on "Histories" and "Prophets." But Buchanan, more enthusiastic every day it seemed, now scoured the scholarly of India to hire William the most able pundits he could find.

Buchanan surprised William even more by advocating an extension of their mission into China. He raised funds for that too. William had learned to seize opportunity when it came. The Serampore Mission soon planned to send two scouts to China, one being Felix. It seemed miraculous when they learned a man named Johannes Lassar was stranded in Calcutta without work. Lassar, who grew up in Macao near China, had been educated in Canton and had completely mastered both the Canton and Mandarin dialects of Chinese! He knew Portuguese and Armenian as well.

"The Lord has opened this particular way for us to China," enthused William. "He intends for us to study under this man first."

Lassar was hired immediately to teach Chinese. His prize pupil turned out not to be Felix but Jabez. Of all William's sons Jabez showed the greatest gift for languages. Jabez was joined in the lessons by Marshman and his oldest son John. The overall goal assigned to Lassar was to aid his students in translating the New Testament into Chinese. Someday the missionaries would arrive in China with a New Testament in hand and the mastery of Chinese on their tongues. This Chinese venture seemed just one more success story for the mission. In the late fall of 1806 the missionaries at Serampore were expecting two additional missionaries from England.

It was Buchanan who bore the bad news. "William, the climate has suddenly changed. I've heard George Barlow is going to send back your new missionaries!"

fourteen

W hat has happened?" gasped William to Buchanan.

"Your enemies have convinced George Barlow that the mutiny in Vellore which cost so many British lives was from resentment of missionaries."

"Vellore? But that's preposterous. I heard the Indian mercenaries mutinied over an order that banned their turbans and forehead marks."

"Perhaps, but Barlow knows Parliament is looking for an excuse to replace him as governor. It's much easier to blame you missionaries than the British army."

The Danish governor Krefting insisted the two newly arrived missionaries were protected under him. Reverend Brown pleaded their case to Barlow. So Barlow allowed them to stay, but his forces soon announced a new restriction on the mission: No more public preaching by missionaries in British territory! The missionaries were stunned. Their evangelism was being shut down by Barlow and his government. What was next? Would William lose his esteemed professorship? He and the other missionaries discussed strategies. They must remain calm. If one door closed they must open another. The Chinese mission would not be ready to launch for several years. But the Burmese mission could be ready in one year.

"Felix, you must begin preparations at once," concluded William.

Another of their strategies was just as bold. If they could not preach in public in British territory they would preach in the asylum of a chapel. Right in downtown Calcutta! And they began raising funds to build a chapel in the area near Lall Bazar. Meanwhile by 1807 the Parliament in London finally pressured the company to replace George Barlow with Lord Minto. Buchanan told William that Minto's government had a first priority of defending India against Napoleon. The insatiable French dictator was now preparing to invade Spain. Would he eventually conquer Russia? If so, would he then storm down into India from the north? Apparently Minto's immediate goal was to establish buffer states around India. But worst of all, Lord Minto seemed receptive to the enemies of the Serampore Mission.

Once again Buchanan brought the news to William. "Lord Minto is going after your press."

"Our press! I can't believe it."

"Someone has told him you are warring with the Hindus and Muslims. You print vicious pamphlets with your press to undermine India's traditional religions. He won't tolerate it. He will send soldiers after it."

William requested an audience with Lord Minto. It was granted. He and Joshua Marshman walked into his office with their arms loaded with their works. The governor asked them to be seated. William presented the governor with a summary of their efforts. They had baptized over one hundred Indians. Many were formally of the upper castes; they were not gullible, uneducated peasants. They showed the governor the volumes of their Bengali Bible. They showed him some of Marshman's translation of the Bible into Chinese. Everything about their presentation was positive.

"As to undermining Indian tradition, your lordship," continued William calmly, "I assure you we honor and respect their traditions. I offer you proof that in no way could be concocted."

"And what is that, sir?"

"A translation from Sanskrit into English that I have labored on for many years—with love and respect. The *Ramayana*. It is the shorter of the two great Sanskrit epics of ancient India, the other being the *Mahabharata,* sir. Still, the *Ramayana* contains twenty-four thousand couplets."

"Yes, I believe I've heard of this story. Isn't this Rama the seventh incarnation of their god Vishnu or something?"

"Yes, sir. And reciting *Ramayana* is considered by the Hindus a religious act, sir. Surely this is proof that I am not hostile to their traditions or religions."

"Perhaps. Wait a moment."

Lord Minto sent for an acquaintance and language expert named Dr. Leyden. Leyden arrived and confirmed that William did indeed have a translation of the Sanskrit epic *Ramayana.*

Lord Minto visibly relaxed. "So you are William Carey, England's language guru, are you?" he commented pleasantly. "What are your latest projects, sir?"

"Your lordship, within the next three years we should finish our complete Bengali Bible as well as New Testaments in Sanskrit, Hindi, Marathi, and Oriya."

"Well done, sir." Lord Minto turned to an orderly. "Rescind that order to confiscate their press."

That same year William received an honorary doctorate of divinity from Brown University in America. But the highlights of 1807 in William's mind were accomplishments of his two older sons. He ordained Felix. Felix was now married and busily planning a mission in Burma, a country hundreds of miles to the east. Besides that, Willy preached for the first time. So William was overjoyed. And although his two younger sons, Jabez, fourteen, and Johnny, eleven, had not yet accepted Christ, William had complete confidence in their spiritual mentors, Ward and the Marshmans.

"After all, they—not I—brought Felix and Willy to Christ," he admitted to himself.

The physical setup of the Serampore Mission continued to prosper. The variety in William's garden astonished visitors. He was something of an expert now on the family Amaryrllidaceae, his favorite example being the daffodil. And in his garden he had built an aviary so large that trees stood freely within it. Birds filled it with song and fluttering color. Many of the birds were described in English for the first time by William. He was also sinking great tanks for aquatic plants. One of his greatest pleasures was receiving seeds, tubers, bulbs, saplings, or even birds from a far-off correspondent, then placing them in his garden. On one occasion, after planting flora he received from England, he shook the "empty" bag over a patch of shaded earth. Days later in that spot he found dear old friends.

"English daisies!" he exclaimed. "What joy. I never expected to see one again."

The garden supplied their communal meals too. The requirements were large now. During the day Mrs. Marshman, whom everyone acknowledged as the "mother" of the mission, saw the following set out: eight large platters of vegetables, four large bowls each of boiled rice and curry, eight good-sized fish or some other meat, three tureens of soup, and nine quarts of milk. On the rest of their property sat numerous buildings now: separate dormitories for girls and boys in the boarding school, a printing building, a warehouse, and residences. Mission House was going to become their church by year's end. Individual families would live in their own houses. The Careys were no exception. Felix would not live there. Leaving his wife behind temporarily, he had gone to Rangoon in Burma. And it was becoming more doubtful that Dolly would live long enough to make the move. For some time she was silenced by a drawn-out fever, similar to the one that killed David Brunsdon. And on December 8, she quietly slipped away.

"How she suffered," said William sadly. "At last she has found peace with the Lord." Then he reflected on a miracle. Through fourteen years of raving, the four sons had never lost their love for their mother. And Dolly's illness had not torn the Careys away from the Placketts. After hearing of Dolly's death Kitty wrote William:

> *I hope my brother will never cease to be my brother, though the ties of nature are broken. I feel a stronger tie than these. . . My love to all the dear children, and to all the friends. Pray write to me, if but two lines. . .*[1]

Death hit the Careys again in 1808. Felix's wife and baby died in childbirth. Felix grieved in Rangoon. He had excited William with his discovery that Pali, the learned language of Burma, was a cousin of Sanskrit in that both languages had descended from the same ancient language. So Felix could attack Pali with great promise.

Not all events that year were sad. Willy was ordained pastor and went north with his wife Mary to work for Ignatius Fernandez in Dinajpour. But he planned to resettle Mudnabati soon after that.

"What do you suppose our old home looks like after so many years?" Willy had often said.

But William had his future in Serampore and Calcutta. Although some whispered it was too soon, he proposed marriage to petite, articulate Charlotte Rumohr. At times invalid, she grew stronger every day in William's company. He had baptized her, taught her English and Bengali, and now married her. She insisted on donating her house in Serampore to the mission. She also insisted on using her dowry to help William's relatives in England, especially William's brother Tom. Tom too was crippled. He had not recovered from his war wounds after all. He could only find work as a night watchman. William knew it was a very dangerous job. So Charlotte sent Tom money to buy a small business.

Then came a visitor. "Peter!" cried William, not believing his eyes.

Completely unconnected to Charlotte's charity, Tom's son Peter arrived in India, not as a missionary but a soldier. He had a ten-year enlistment in a cavalry regiment, the 24th Light Dragoons. News that his father might buy a small business surprised Peter. He informed William that seventy-one-year-old grandfather Edmund was healthy. Then with great enthusiasm he informed William that every nephew and niece of "Uncle William" dreamed of coming one day to India!

"Others will follow me," Peter assured him.

William was embarrassed. Was he some kind of hero back in Northamptonshire? That was the last thing he wished. In fact he wrote Andrew Fuller once that if he died before Fuller died he wished no adulation from the mission society. He was but a loiterer, a halfhearted servant. Yes, he had translated a lot, but so much more remained to translate. Good heavens, he hadn't even finished his dictionaries in Bengali and Marathi yet. And besides, he loved his work.

On January 1, 1809, the mission opened their chapel on Lall Bazar. The stately building could have sat in the Clapham suburb of London with its eight great columns in front. Its entry was a long paved walk with gardens on both sides. Marshman had tirelessly worked on raising the thirty thousand rupees the chapel had cost. William shared the first sermon with Nathaniel Forsyth, the London Missionary Society's only missionary in India. William rented rooms nearby, so he could pastor the chapel in the evenings.

William knew all too well his own shortcomings as a preacher. To John Ryland he confided:

> *Marshman is all keenness for God's work. Often have I seen him, when we have been walking together, eye a group of persons, like a hawk, and go up to try on them the Gospel's utmost strength. I have known him engage with such for hours, more eager for the contest when he left off than when he began. It has filled me with shame. In point of zeal he is a Luther, I an Erasmus. Ward, too, has such a faculty of addressing things to the heart, and his thoughts run so naturally in this channel, that he fixes the minds of all who hear him; whilst I, after repeated efforts, can scarcely get out a few dry sentences, and, if rebuffed at the*

*beginning, sit like a silly mute, and scarcely say
anything at all. Yet I do desire to give myself, such
as I am, to the cause of God, and to be wholly
employed in His service. None stands more in
need than I of the prayers of God's people. . .[2]*

Shortcomings or not, that summer it seemed to William
that for him India was over. On June 26, 1809, he went to bed
with a fever. The next day it was much worse. He waited
for the chills to strike him but only the fever raged over his
body. This was not a recurrence of jungle fever that could be
calmed by quinine. Soon he was dreaming. God sent him to
all government-run churches. There he informed gaping clerics to sell their churches to the first body of Nonconformists
who had the money. His dream was delicious. Mighty angels
accompanied him.

"Oh, yes, and before I forget it," he would add in the
dream, "the Lord wishes war banished. All soldiers are to be
mustered out immediately."

Once in awhile he awoke to what seemed reality. Charlotte
or Ward or Jabez or Johnny or the Marshmans would be dab-
bing a wet cloth at his forehead or forcing him to drink fruit
juice or broth. Once he heard someone say few Englishmen
lived twenty years in India, as if they were resigned to his
death. But he dreamed less and less. Finally his fever was
gone and he lay in unwilling torpor.

"I would like to attack a page of Sanskrit," he mumbled
one day to wife Charlotte.

She laughed. "I know now you will recover."

Soon he was back on his feet. Repercussions were eventually heard from England. None too subtle, John Ryland sent

funds to have his portrait painted. "Before it is too late," mused William, not morbidly but almost longingly. How he wished to join the Lord—when the Lord decided his work was finished, of course. Someday he would have his portrait painted as Ryland and the mission society wished. When he had time. At Serampore he was now baptizing one to three converts every Sunday. He had his garden with its aviaries and ponds to tend. He had his classes at Fort William College. He had the chapel at Lall Bazar to pastor. Translations and printings were steaming full speed ahead again.

"Print shop is a misnomer," he told his chief printer Ward. "Your 'shop' is a factory."

The building for the printing was more than one hundred seventy feet long. Over fifty men labored in the building. There ran not one press now but five. Ward had his own small office. Outside his office was another with pundits at their desks, translating. Farther on were cases full of precious type for the scripts of Bengali, Nagari, Marathi, Persian, Arabic, Telugu, Punjabi, Oriya, Kanarese, Chinese, Burmese, Greek, Hebrew, and English. Several men were engaged proofing. A few men made only ink. Numerous men manned the presses. From the presses men gathered the pages and folded them before taking them to the six men who bound the pages. Beyond all that were the type casters and further yet, partly in the open, was a paper mill where they manufactured most of their paper. Reams of higher quality paper were imported from England too. Type and paper were stored in the long building, but most manuscripts awaiting typesetting and printing were stored in a separate warehouse nearby.

In 1811 Felix remarried, this time to a woman born in

Burma to English parents. Willy joined the mission's very industrious John Chamberlain at Katwa, less than sixty miles north of Serampore. Willy was not sorry to leave Mudnabati after being gored by a wild buffalo. In November 1811 William's pretty niece Phoebe, Ann Hobson's daughter, arrived in Serampore. Her big news from England was that William's nephew Eustace, son of brother Tom, was now preaching the Gospel. Charlotte welcomed her as a member of the household. Lively Phoebe made her a wonderful companion. Jabez, dutiful but not yet in Christ, was in Calcutta studying law. Johnny was the only son at home, but he was out working all day. Phoebe was entranced by the house. For the first time in a long time William was made to realize just how different their Indian homes were. There were no chimneys or fireplaces. Rooms were many and spacious. Ceilings were twenty feet high. Windows were huge but not glassed.

The year 1812 was not the tranquil year 1811 had been. Word came that Napoleon had either conquered or forced an alliance with nearly every country of Europe. His long-dreaded attack of Russia seemed imminent. Of course that meant he was that much closer to attacking India. As if Britain didn't have enough to worry about they were sparring with America again. And it was common knowledge now that George III was mentally ill. The fate of the Serampore Mission seemed no better that year. In the first three months of 1812 five died, including Ward's six-year-old daughter and the Marshmans's baby boy.

"What can happen next?" asked William sadly.

On March 12 he was just rising in his rooms near the Lall Bazar chapel when Joshua Marshman burst in. His face was ashen.

"Not another death!" gasped William.

"It's the print building. . ."

"Fire?" asked William in a weak voice.

"Yes."

fifteen

"Praise God, no lives are lost," said William numbly.

"Yes, praise God," replied Marshman.

"Which manuscripts did we lose?" asked William dully. Everything but lives was replaceable—at a cost of money or time. But manuscripts could be replaced only by much precious time.

"I'm afraid we lost all your grammars and dictionaries."

"I can't replace those in a year's work."

" 'Every branch that beareth fruit, he purgeth it, that it may bring forth more fruit,' " said Marshman quietly.

"Yes, of course. The Lord Himself says that in the Book of John. And so I will 'be still and know that the Lord is God.' "

William later estimated the loss at sixty thousand rupees. The presses were saved. All four thousand of the type punches were saved. All nearby buildings were unscathed. Hundreds of boys and girls now boarded at the Marshmans's schools. The missionaries had much to be thankful for. But the print building was lost, as was an enormous amount of supplies, including a very large shipment of English paper. Three-quarters of a million sheets of superb paper were now ashes.

A few months later Jabez, the dutiful but unconvinced son, finally came to Christ. He gave up law and prepared himself to shepherd the heathen at some location not yet known.

Johnny was preaching but William was not sure Christ was in his head or his heart. Lord Minto's government in Calcutta still was erratic in its attitude toward missionaries. They refused entry to the first missionary from America, Adoniram Judson.

William offered him an alternative. "I suggest Burma. My son Felix is already there in Rangoon. There is much to be done."

Later that year, William, at fifty-one, finally sat for his portrait. Robert Home, distinguished enough to have painted Wellesley, was the artist. William insisted the theme of the portrait be his translating. So the artist portrayed William, pen in hand, at a table with his pundit. Several books are evident beside a manuscript on which William supposedly toils although his eyeglasses are set aside. The words on the manuscript are "we do hear them speak in our tongues the wonderful works of God" from the Book of Acts—but in Sanskrit! For that reason only William liked the portrait very much. His own likeness disappointed him. He appeared bland and bald with dainty white hands, a mousy clerk who had never suffered in his life. How false the portrait was. Or was it?

"God knows I have not done enough," he reflected.

The next year was momentous. Because of the fire the Mission Society in England had rallied as never before to raise funds. Money poured in to the Serampore Mission. In global matters, Britain, ruled by Parliament and George III's son, was at war with America again. Fortunately Napoleon had been routed by the Russians. His army was in tatters and his empire was unraveling. The withdrawal of that imminent danger from India drew attention from the Crown. Would there be another new governor?

Buchanan as usual brought William the news. "Francis Rawdon-Hastings, Earl of Moira, will be our new governor. No relation to the Hastings that governed India years ago. This Hastings is a military man, but I believe as in the case of Cornwallis his purpose is not military but to make money."

"Money. What does this mean for missions?" asked William.

"You will benefit, I think. I hear the Claphamites are very strong in England now. Wilberforce has spoken very highly of you in Parliament. It seems the fire has made every educated person in England aware of your accomplishments."

"Me? Really?"

"And there's been another development. For the first time the Crown is sending to India a bishop of the Church of England and three archdeacons."

In 1814 William saw portions of speeches made in the English Parliament the previous year during many days of debate over India. Three whole days were spent debating the desirability of missionaries in India. The Claphamite, and now esteemed thirty-year member of the House of Commons, William Wilberforce said:

> *These "Anabaptist" missionaries, as among other low epithets they have been contemptuously called, are entitled to our highest respect and admiration. One of them, Dr. Carey, was originally in one of the lowest social stations; but with all its disadvantages, he had the genius as well as the benevolence to devise a plan, which has since been pursued, of forming a society for communicating the blessings of our Christian light to the*

187

native peoples of India.

His first care was to qualify himself to act a distinguished part in this truly noble enterprise. He resolutely bent himself to the study of languages. After reaching considerable proficiency in these, he applied himself to several of the oriental tongues, more especially to that which, I understand, is the parent of them all, the Sanskrit, in which his proficiency is acknowledged to be greater than. . .any other European. Of several of these languages he has already published a grammar; of one or two of them a dictionary, and he has in contemplation a still greater literary enterprise. The very plan of these would excite the highest admiration and respect in every unprejudiced mind.

All the time, Sir, he is laboring as a missionary with a warmth of zeal only equalled by that with which he prosecutes his literary labors. Merit like this could not escape the distinguishing eye of Lord Wellesley, who appointed him Professor of Sanskrit and Bengali in the college at Calcutta. . .[1]

In the House of Lords Richard Wellesley echoed the praise:

. . .whilst I was in India, I never knew of any danger arising from the missionaries' proceedings. the greatest number of them were in the Danish settlement of Serampore. Some of them were very learned men, particularly Dr. Carey, whom I employed in the College of Fort William.

I always considered the missionaries who were in India in my time a quiet, ordered, discreet, and learned body. . .[2]

A resolution was passed by Parliament that read:

That it is the duty of this country to promote the interest and happiness of the inhabitants of the British Dominion in India, and that such means ought to be adopted as may lead to the introduction among them of useful knowledge, and of religious and moral improvement. That in furtherance of the above objects sufficient facilities should be afforded by law to persons desirous of going to and remaining in India for the purpose of accomplishing these beneficent designs.[3]

Buchanan was almost as stunned as William. "I think it's safe to assume your missionary work will now flourish. And now we know why the Church of England has finally arrived here in force."

And flourish the missionaries did under the new resolution. By the end of 1813 the Serampore Mission had two hundred workers keeping ten presses busy! Also, Jabez had been invited to do mission work in the Moluccan Islands, recently taken from the Dutch. From his very old days of compiling data William remembered the islands as the "Spice Islands." He counseled Jabez for weeks about missionary work in the Moluccas, even about how to ship back to Serampore bulbs and tubers and seeds and cuttings of interesting plants in the Moluccas. And last but not least he counseled Jabez on marriage.

"Don't be content to bear yourself toward your wife with propriety but let love be the spring of your conduct. Esteem her highly, so that she will esteem you highly. Yet, remember that love arising from physical beauty will wear off and that lasting love must come from character."

"Of course, Father. Pray that I give my all to God with a heart of sincerity."

Then in three busy days in January 1814 Jabez was ordained a pastor, married, and shipped off with his bride to the Moluccas!

"Praise the Lord," an overjoyed William told Charlotte as the ship sailed. "Let us exalt His name together. He has been so gracious to us. We have three of four sons engaged in the active spread of the Gospel and two in new countries!"

William received a letter from nephew Peter written in Cawnpore in July of 1814. His horse had fallen on him and shattered his leg. But worse yet, he was fighting a severe infection. A letter followed that was like a bombshell; Peter had died two days after he had written the letter! William had to give that tragic news to Peter's younger brother Eustace, who arrived in India just days later. Then William wrote his condolences to brother Tom.

Eustace Carey was only one of five new missionaries now at the Serampore Mission sent by the mission society in England. But the new popularity of the missionary work back in England had wrought an ironic twist. The society now wanted to dictate to the mission in Serampore. Each new missionary had already been assigned a certain task. Yates was to assist William with translating. Penney was to assist Marshman in the schools. Pearce was to assist Ward with the printing.

And the new missionaries considered their only authority the society in England. There was hardly anyone back at the society William could complain to. John Sutcliffe had died. And the most powerful society member of all, bulldog Andrew Fuller, at sixty, was sick and dying. It grieved William to think of these wonderful old men passing on, realizing with a start that the young missionaries thought of him as one of these old men too.

The situation worsened.

"Good heavens," cried William to Ward and Marshman. "The society is now sending directions as to which missions over here should be initiated and which closed! Fuller understood that the society cannot make decisions about India from England when it takes six months for a question to be asked, then six months for the question to be answered. How well I remember a line of wisdom from one of his early letters: 'We here in England never intend to govern; the distance is too great for you to await our directions.' "

In 1815 William learned Felix and his family had been in an accident in Burma several months before. They had been aboard a ship that capsized. His wife and two small children drowned. Felix was profoundly discouraged, thinking of giving up the ministry for civil service. Then William learned that Andrew Fuller had died. It was a real struggle for him to keep his spirits up.

That same year Britain had broken off its war with America. Napoleon had regrouped to make an effort to reconquer Europe but was defeated at Waterloo by combined forces of Austria, Prussia, Russia, and Britain. The British general was none other than Arthur Wellesley, who had already won the title Duke of Wellington. He was now a great national hero of

Britain. The ascendancy of the Wellesleys certainly would not hurt the missionary cause. But popularity was a double-edged sword.

"I find myself now almost longing for the old days of 'neglect,'" commented Ward after an especially trying day with the five new missionaries.

Just as the Serampore Mission now labored with strained cooperation, so it seemed did the rest of India. Governor Hastings, whose time in India was meant to stabilize the country and increase profits, found himself instead diverted into conducting war against Ghurkas invading from the north, then warring against the always hostile Marathas in central India. In fact, some critics now said Britain could hold India only by force. William did not know.

"I did not come to bring India to George III, but to Christ," he commented.

The situation at Serampore worsened. Some of the new missionaries had written England that the older missionaries were feathering their nests, especially the Marshmans. Joshua Marshman was furious; William was heartbroken. Dolly and his son Peter were dead. Felix was confused and broken, wandering somewhere in Assam far to the northeast. Two sons labored for the mission society, each one self-sufficient. Willy he now considered the most diligent missionary in India. How dimly the society in England understood their personal sacrifices in India. But even more depressing was that these new missionaries saw the austere lives of the older missionaries with their own eyes and still didn't understand. William tried to explain to them that not he but the Marshmans had always been the ones who greeted or entertained visitors. That was why they had finer furnishings in their house than did any of the others.

"Finer it most certainly is," was the cynical comment heard from Eustace Carey, William's own nephew, and yet the most headstrong and critical of the newcomers.

By 1818 the situation was so much worse the younger missionaries pulled out of Serampore. They settled in the Entally area of Calcutta and formed the "Calcutta Missionary Union." They began to create a second Serampore mission, presses and all! They even started a church that would compete with the Lall Bazar chapel. But those betrayals seemed mild compared to their continual vendetta against Marshman. William fumed. Didn't the young upstarts realize the Marshmans brought over two thousand rupees a month into the common coffer with their schools?

After four years of this aggravation from the younger missionaries William wrote to one of the members of the mission society in England:

> *I do not think I am blind to his (Marshman's) faults. I have seen all his so-called "tortuousities" and every other defect with which he is charged. But I cannot caricature him, as I am sure our brethren do. . . . I believe him to be one of the firmest friends the Mission ever had. . .*[4]

And to another member he wrote: "I do not recollect in my whole life anything which has given me so much distress as this schism. . ."[5]

Those were powerful words from a man who had lived fourteen tragic years with a raging, insane wife. To aggravate him even more Jabez had returned to Serampore because the

Dutch had taken over the Molucca Islands again; they allowed no Nonconformist missionaries. William loved his son but he was deeply wounded when Jabez began to criticize Marshman too. That just proved to William how insidious such unjust talk was.

sixteen

/n 1818 William was cheered by two developments. Although Ward returned to England for a short stay, he had first gone to Chittagong and counseled Felix. And Felix responded to his "spiritual father." Now the prodigal was back in Serampore, recuperating. William hoped to soon have him back in Christ's fold and preaching. The second note of cheer was a project that William had kept in the back of his mind for over twenty years. He and the ever-optimistic John Thomas had discussed it. William now focused on this grand project, possibly his last novel experiment. At fifty-six he was quite old for a European who had been in the tropics for twenty-three years.

"It's high time we establish our own college at Serampore, brothers," William told Ward and Marshman.

Money poured in for the enterprise. Donors ranged from venerable Charles Grant to Lord Hastings himself. Eight acres of land were purchased nearby. The main building was not expected to be finished until 1821. But they began their classes in 1819 anyway. The purpose of the college was to instruct the Indians, in Bengali, in history, geography, astronomy, and divinity. From these students would come their ordained Indian preachers of tomorrow. It was bold beyond the ambitions of even those sympathetic to such a cause. But after all, they already instructed ten thousand young students in various free schools within twenty miles of Serampore.

"The best of these literate youngsters will be candidates for our college," reasoned William. "And, of course, we will accept any others who can qualify."

William also continued his pursuit of botany. He had long wanted to join a horticultural society in Calcutta but there was none, a staggering omission in a land abounding in tropical plants. He deemed himself too much of an amateur to start one himself but finally Lady Hastings insisted that he should organize it. "Who has better credentials for taking on the impossible?" she asked. So he solicited interest, then announced a first meeting for September 1820. The following year Lord Hastings gave land to the growing botanical society for experiments. Roxburgh, now back in England, sponsored William's membership in the Royal Horticultural Society.

"And he writes that I'm sure to be elected a fellow in the prestigious Linnean Society," said William, shaking his head at what he considered such undeserved rewards.

But as much as he loved plants he always returned to his translations, and his classes at Fort William College. The grand plan he had described to Reverend Brown many years before was well along. He had virtually promised complete Bibles in Sanskrit, Bengali, Punjabi, Hindi, Oriya, Marathi, Gujarati, Telugu, and Kanarese. Nine languages. "Good heavens!" had been Brown's reaction. By 1820 William had delivered five complete Bibles: Sanskrit, Bengali, Hindi, Oriya, and Marathi. And he had partials of all the others.

"And Chinese too!" he reminded himself.

The Serampore Mission still required much from William. In 1820 he met with the young missionaries in Calcutta. He said as firmly as he could that all of them had suffered from pride and it was time to end the schism. He felt great peace afterwards because it seemed the battle was over. And his sons seemed settled. At Serampore the rejuvenated Felix labored. Willy continued his ministry in Katwa. Jabez had gone to Ajmer in central India, armed with Hindi Bibles. Johnny, though uncommitted to Christ, at least had a good job in Calcutta as a civil servant.

But in the midst of all the calm tiny Charlotte slowly weakened. For several years she enjoyed almost normal health, but by early 1821, at sixty, she was very frail. William carried her into the garden every day to enjoy its sweet smells and happy sounds. But finally in May Charlotte passed away. William grieved again. Their marriage had lasted thirteen years.

For many years, even though bedridden and crippled like his sister Polly, Charlotte too had been a faithful correspondent.

"The relatives in England mourn for her like a sister," said William, reading a letter of condolence. "How she touched them."

William knew the loss of Charlotte was irreparable. She was the love of his life. But little did he realize how much more grief lay in the months ahead. Krishna Pal, indefatigable preacher who had converted many of his countrymen, was lost in a twinkling to cholera. Then Felix, who had fought a fever for many months, died at only thirty-seven. A few months later Ward, at fifty-four, succumbed to cholera. That same year William fell on a ghat in darkness and so severely injured his leg he could not walk for four months. He walked again but with a limp.

Psalm 6 expressed his anguish perfectly, "Have mercy

upon me, O Lord; for I am weak: O Lord, heal me; for my bones are vexed. My soul is also sore vexed: but thou, O Lord, how long?"

William could barely bring himself to acknowledge the arrival of a new governor, always a great event. Ships clogged the Hooghly. Cannons boomed. Fireworks lit the night sky. Hastings, who had governed India for ten years, was leaving. Once sparkling and debonair, he had been reduced by India to a whisper. In his last years only his wife had given the governor's house any brilliance. Charlotte had been the same way, reflected William.

"The new governor will be Lord Amherst," Buchanan told him.

Still William labored on. God would heal him if it was His will. Was there ever enough time for William to do what had to be done? When he had risen after his grave illness of 1809 Ward had joked, "And the machine works on." And William did so once again. He even remarried. His wife was Grace Hughes, a widow about fifteen years younger than himself.

In 1826 Joshua Marshman returned to England. To William's dismay he learned Marshman there again encountered accusations of feathering his nest in India. Nephew Eustace Carey had returned to England to throw fuel on the fire. Apparently the truce with the young missionaries was broken. None of the main old founders of the mission society lived. John Ryland had died in 1823. The intrusion of the society into the Serampore Mission never irritated William more. The society's reassurances that William was as pure as snow and that it was only the scoundrel Marshman who was tainted infuriated him. Marshman was as poor as he was. And either man could have accumulated great wealth in India, but gave everything to the Serampore Mission. Even a letter from his innocent sisters now hinted of Marshman's villainy.

"I was a party to all his public actions and writings," stormed William. "I detest all these mean accusations against him. There is a proverb: 'Thine own friend and thy father's friend, forsake not.' "

Angrily he wrote the mission society to refuse all future assistance. At the age of sixty-six he was severing the Serampore Mission's long bond with the very society he helped create!

seventeen

A haggard Marshman returned to Serampore in 1829. "I know what you're thinking, William," he said. "I am only sixty-one, yet look seventy. And look at you. You are nearly seventy, yet look sixty. You're as stable as a great old tree: white stockings, tan knee pants, white waistcoat, white jacket, and black hat. You look just as you did twenty-nine years ago. Why, you are even walking well again."

"You sir, look like Job. Yet you have endured. I prayed all the while you were in England that you would remain a thousand times more temperate than I felt."

"And how is our new governor, Lord William Bentinck?" asked Marshman, for there was yet another new governor.

"I have great news, friend. Our pleas have worked on some English consciences after all. Apparently Governor Bentinck will soon give me a declaration to translate into Bengali. He is banning sati!"

"Hallelujah! No more widow burning. Praise the Lord."

William was now too moved to speak. Sati had haunted him for a long time. Hundreds of widows were burned every year. The practice jumped directly into his face time after time. He didn't know which was more heartbreaking: news that one widow who was burned alive was a mere girl of eleven or news that thirty-three wives of a dead maharajah in Rajput had all burned at one time! And what of the horrifying stories of widows who had a change of heart but were forced back into the fire!

After a long silence Marshman said, "I do not want to remain alienated from the mission society in England. . ."

"But the terrible accusations. . ."

"I've heard all the objections. Some may have merit. Much of the property is in our names."

"But that was only because the mission society itself had no legal presence here."

"Still, it can probably be remedied now with legal help. Why can't Johnny help us? He's a lawyer in Calcutta now."

So Johnny did do the legal work. Over the months the missionaries transferred all their property to the society. It seemed now that William and the Marshmans really had given their all to the mission society.

Calcutta had a severe banking crisis in which the savings of many institutions and individuals vanished. Fort William College also suffered, and released William in his thirtieth year of service. The Serampore Mission lost its savings too.

The summer of 1833 William suffered lethargy from the heat as never before. His activity was reduced to a crawl. Then, one month after turning seventy-three, William was hammered by a stroke. Yet he endured. In November he reflected that he had now lived in India forty years. And what had he, a pitiful little worm, accomplished? In forty years the mission had probably converted only a few thousand Indians. And he had not kept his rash promise to Brown. Of the complete Bible in nine languages he had delivered only six. Still, he had compiled many dictionaries and grammars. Oh, yes, the New Testament was available in thirty languages, or was it thirty-one? And someone had said their presses had printed over two hundred thousand different items in forty languages. But many others had helped him—just as the Marshmans had created the mission's more than one hundred schools that educated thousands of Indian children. Of course there were the thousands of civil servants William had educated at Fort William College, and hopefully instilled a sense of debt to Christ. And there was the mission's own college with its goal of educating Indians. And he did found the horticultural society. He and Marshman probably had something to do with eliminating sati. Perhaps William had been helpful in eliminating child sacrifice too. He hoped so.

"Who knows but God?"

Visitors told William he did more. They said his *Enquiry into the Obligations of Christians to Use Means for the Conversion of the Heathens* laid the foundations for all future mission work. They said the Serampore Compact was a model for every modern Protestant mission. They said the magnitude of his translation work put him in the company of Jerome, Luther, Wycliffe, and Tyndale. They mentioned he was a fellow in the Linnaean Society.

One day he used his meager remaining energy to admonish a visitor who had repeated praise too often. "Dr. Carey this, Dr. Carey that!" cried William. "Please, sir, after I am gone, praise nothing about Dr. Carey. Praise only Dr. Carey's Savior!"

He did not revel in good works. How could a man who had translated the New Testament so many times not know salvation was gained only by faith and God's grace? The cool season of little rain revived him a little. But when the hot weather came again in the summer of 1834 with its heavy rain he wilted. He could no longer move. He couldn't eat.

He couldn't speak. Grace tended him. Willy appeared from Katwa. Jabez came from Ajmer. Johnny was there. Sunday morning of June 8 Joshua Marshman visited him just before leaving to conduct services at Lall Bazar chapel in Calcutta. William drank in the vision of his old friend. He was sure he would never see Marshman again in this life.

William was resigned, even content. The Lord awaited him. Ever the organizer, he left instructions to be buried next to Charlotte. His epitaph he took from lines penned by Isaac Watts—lines that greatly pleased him:

> *A wretched, poor, and helpless worm,*
> *On Thy kind arms I fall.*

William Carey died at sunrise June 9, 1834.

Further Reading

Beck, James R., *Dorothy Carey: The Tragic and Untold Story of Mrs. William Carey*. Grand Rapids, Mich.: Baker Book House, 1992.

Carey, S. Pearce, *William Carey, D.D., Fellow of the Linnean Society*. London: Hodder & Stoughton Ltd. 1923. Reprint, London: Wakeman Trust, 1993.

Carey, William, *An Enquiry into the Obligations of Christians to Use Means for the Conversion of the Heathens*. Leicester: Ann Ireland, 1792.

Finnie, Kellsye, *William Carey: By Trade a Cobbler*. London: Kingsway Publications, 1986.

Gardner, Brian, *The East India Company*. New York: McCall Publishing Company, 1971.

George, Timothy, *Faithful Witness: Life and Mission of William Carey*. Birmingham, Ala.: New Hope, 1991.

Moorhouse, Geoffrey, *India Britannica*. New York: Harper & Row, Publishers, 1983.

Moorhouse, Geoffrey, *The Missionaries*. Philadelphia and New York: J. B. Lippincott Company, 1973.

Potts, E. Daniel, *British Baptist Missionaries in India, 1793-1837: History of Serampore and Its Missions*. Cambridge: Cambridge University Press, 1967.

Robinson, Francis, ed., *Cambridge Encyclopedia of India*. Cambridge: Cambridge University Press, 1989.

ACKNOWLEDGMENTS

Barbour Publishing, Inc. expresses their appreciation to all those who generously gave permission to reprint copyrighted material. Diligent effort has been made to identify, locate, contact, and secure permission to use copyrighted material. If any permissions or acknowledgments have been inadvertently omitted or if such permissions were not received by the time of publication, the publisher would sincerely appreciate receiving complete information so that correct credit can be given in future editions.

Chapter 5
[1] Excerpts from "letter of William Carey to his father, November 12, 1790," taken from the volume of letters 1787-1814, William Carey Collection. Reprinted by permission of Regents Park College Oxford (Angus Library), Oxford, England.
[2] Excerpts from the pamphlet *An Enquiry into the Obligations of Christians to Use Means for the Conversion of the Heathens in which the Religious State of the Different Nations of the World, the Success of Former Undertakings, and the Practicability of Further Undertakings are Considered* by William Carey taken from *William Carey* by S. Pearce Carey (ed. Peter Masters). Wakeman Trust, London, 1993.
[3] Excerpts from *William Carey* by S. Pearce Carey (ed. Peter Masters). Wakeman Trust, London, 1993.
[4] Ibid.

Chapter 6
[1] Excerpts from the "Association resolution of 1792" in *William Carey, D.D., Fellow of the Linnean Society* by S. Pearce Carey. London: Hodder & Stoughton, Ltd., 1923.
[2] Excerpts from the "Society resolution of 1792" in *William Carey, D.D., Fellow of the Linnean Society* by S. Pearce Carey. London: Hodder & Stoughton, Ltd., 1923.
[3] Excerpts from "William Carey Collection." Reprinted by permission of the Baptist Missionary Society.
[4] Excerpts from *William Carey* by S. Pearce Carey (ed. Peter Masters). Wakeman Trust, London, 1993.

Chapter 8
[1] Excerpts from the journal entries of William Carey are taken from *Dorothy Carey: The Tragic and Untold Story of Mrs. William Carey* by James R. Beck. Grand Rapids, Michigan: Baker Book House, 1992.
[2] Excerpts from "letter of William Carey to John Sutcliffe," taken from *Dorothy Carey: The Tragic and Untold Story of Mrs. William Carey* by James R. Beck. Grand Rapids, Michigan: Baker Book House, 1992.

Chapter 9
[1] Excerpts from the journal entries of William Carey are taken from *Dorothy Carey: The Tragic and Untold Story of Mrs. William Carey* by James R. Beck. Grand Rapids, Michigan: Baker Book House, 1992.
[2] Excerpts from the "journal entry of March or April 1794," are taken from *William Carey, D.D., Fellow of the Linnean Society* by S. Pearce Carey. London: Hodder & Stoughton, Ltd., 1923.

[3] Excerpts from the journal entries of William Carey are taken from *Dorothy Carey: The Tragic and Untold Story of Mrs. William Carey* by James R. Beck. Grand Rapids, Michigan: Baker Book House, 1992.

[4] Ibid.

Chapter 10

[1] Excerpts from the journal entries of William Carey are taken from *Dorothy Carey: The Tragic and Untold Story of Mrs. William Carey* by James R. Beck. Grand Rapids, Michigan: Baker Book House, 1992.

[2] Ibid.

[3] Ibid.

[4] Ibid.

[5] Ibid.

[6] Excerpts from "William Carey Collection." Reprinted by permission of the Baptist Missionary Society.

Chapter 11

[1] Excerpts from the letters of William Carey are taken from *Dorothy Carey: The Tragic and Untold Story of Mrs. William Carey* by James R. Beck. Grand Rapids, Michigan: Baker Book House, 1992.

[2] Ibid.

[3] Excerpts from the letters of William Carey are taken from *William Carey, D.D., Fellow of the Linnean Society* by S. Pearce Carey. London: Hodder & Stoughton, Ltd., 1923.

[4] Ibid.

Chapter 12

[1] Excerpts from the "letter from William Ward to William Carey" are taken from *William Carey, D.D., Fellow of the Linnean Society* by S. Pearce Carey. London: Hodder & Stoughton, Ltd., 1923.

[2] Excerpts from the letters of William Carey are taken from *Dorothy Carey: The Tragic and Untold Story of Mrs. William Carey* by James R. Beck. Grand Rapids, Michigan: Baker Book House, 1992.

Chapter 14

[1] Excerpts from the "letter from Kitty in Clipston to William Carey" are taken from *Dorothy Carey: The Tragic and Untold Story of Mrs. William Carey* by James R. Beck. Grand Rapids, Michigan: Baker Book House, 1992.

[2] Excerpts from the letters of William Carey are taken from *William Carey, D.D., Fellow of the Linnean Society* by S. Pearce Carey. London: Hodder & Stoughton, Ltd., 1923.

Chapter 15

[1] Excerpts from the letters of William Carey are taken from *William Carey, D.D., Fellow of the Linnean Society* by S. Pearce Carey. London: Hodder & Stoughton, Ltd., 1923.

[2] Ibid.

[3] Excerpts from *William Carey* by S. Pearce Carey (ed. Peter Masters). Wakeman Trust, London, 1993.

[4] Ibid.

[5] Ibid.